Stations and Lines:

27 Nishi-takashimadaira
26 Shin-takashimadaira
25 Takashimadaira
24 Nishidai
23 Hasune
22 Motohasunuma
21 Shimura-sakaue
20 Motohasunuma
19 Shin-itabashi
18 Itabashi-kuyakushomae
17 Nishi-sugamo

Shimura-sanchome
Shin-itabashi
Nishi-sugamo
Shin-koshinzuka

Thru to Urawa-misono
Saitama Railway Line

Shimo
Oji-kamiya
Oji-ekimae

19 Akabane-iwabuchi
18 Shimo
17 Oji-kamiya
16 Oji
15
14
13 Hon-komagome
12 Todai-mae

Akabane
Akabane-iwabuchi

Wakoshi
01 Wakoshi
02 Chikatetsu-narimasu
03 Chikatetsu-akatsuka
04 Heiwadai
05 Hikawadai
06 Kotake-mukaihara
07 Senkawa
08 Kanamecho

Tobu Tojo Line
Fukutoshin Line

37 Toshimaen
36 Nerima
35 Shin-egota
34 Ochiai-minami-nagasaki
33 Nakai

Seibu Ikebukuro Line

Ogikubo
Shin-koenji
Higashi-koenji
Shin-nakano
Nakano-fujimicho
Nakano-shimbashi
Nishi-shinjuku-gochome

Chuo Line
01 Nakano
02 Shin-nakano
03 Higashi-koenji
04 Shin-koenji
05 Higashi-nakano

01 Nakai
02 Ochiai

07 Nakano-sakaue
08 Nishi-shinjuku

06 Tochomae
29 Nishi-shinjuku-gochome

Ikebukuro
09 25 Ikebukuro

Marunouchi Line
Yamanote Line

Sengawa
Kanamecho

Takadanobaba
02 Takadanobaba
03 Waseda

Higashi-ikebukuro
24 Higashi-ikebukuro
23 Gokokuji
22 Edogawabashi

Higashi-ikebukuro 4-chome
Shin-otsuka
Myogadani
Hakusan
Korakuen

15 Sugamo
14 Sengoku
13 Hakusan
12 Korakuen
11 Myogadani

Otsuka-ekimae
Otsuka

Mejiro
Higashi-ikebukuro
Waseda
Gokokuji

Chuo Line
01 Ogikubo
02 Minami-asagaya
03 Shin-koenji
04 Higashi-koenji
05 Shin-nakano
06 30 Nakano

31 Nakano-sakaue

Higashi-nakano
Nakai

02 Ochiai
03 Takadanobaba
04 Waseda
05 Kagurazaka
06 Iidabashi

Tozai Line
Shin-okubo
Wakamatsu-kawada

Ushigome-yanagicho
Ushigome-kagurazaka

04 Ushigome-yanagicho
05 Ushigome-kagurazaka

Kagurazaka

06 Iidabashi
10 Iidabashi
13 Iidabashi

Jimbocho

Akebonobashi
Higashi-shinjuku
Shinjuku-gyoemmae
Yotsuya

Shinjuku
08 Shinjuku
27 Shinjuku

28 Nishi-shinjuku-gochome

03 Shinjuku-sanchome
04 Yotsuya-sanchome

10 Shinjuku-gyoemmae
11 Shinjuku-sanchome
12 Yotsuya-sanchome

08 Shinjuku
13 Yotsuya

04 Ichigaya
05 Ichigaya

Kudanshita
05 Kudanshita

Tochomae
27 Tochomae

26 Yoyogi
Yoyogi

Sendagaya
Shinanomachi
Kokuritsu-kyogijo
Meiji-jingumae

Kojimachi
15 Kojimachi
Hanzomon

01 Yoyogi-uehara
02 Yoyogi-koen

Harajuku

Keio Line
Keio Inokashira Line

Meidaimae
Sasazuka

Shimo-kitazawa

03 Meiji-jingumae

24 Aoyama-itchome
03 Aoyama-itchome
04 Aoyama-itchome

Akasaka-mitsuke
Nagata

07 Aoyama-itchome
04 Akasaka-mitsuke
05 Akasaka-mitsuke

Gaiemmae
03 Gaiemmae

05 Nogizaka

Tameike-sanno
06 Tameike-sanno
05 Tameike-sanno

Shibuya
01 Shibuya
01 Shibuya

Hanzomon Line

01 Omote-sando
02 04 Omote-sando

05 Nogizaka

Akasaka
05 Akasaka

Roppongi-itchome
05 Roppongi-itchome

Naka-meguro
01 Naka-meguro

Ebisu
02 Ebisu

Hiro-o
03 Hiro-o

Roppongi
04 Roppongi
23 Roppongi

Kamiyacho
05 Kamiyacho

Azabu-juban
04 Azabu-juban
05 Azabu-juban

Ginza Line

Hibiya Line

Tokyu Den-en-toshi Line
Tokyu Oimachi Line
Tokyu Toyoko Line
Tokyu Meguro Line

Jiyugaoka
Den-en-chofu
Ookayama
Hatanodai

Meguro
01 Meguro
03 Meguro

Shirokanedai
02 Shirokanedai

Shirokane-takanawa
03 Shirokane-takanawa

Mita
04 Mita
05 Mita

Sengakuji
07 Sengakuji

01 Nishi-magome
02 Magome
03 Nakanobu
04 Togoshi
05 Gotanda
06 Takanawadai

Gotanda
04 Gotanda

Osaki
Shinagawa
Oimachi
Tamachi

Takanawadai

Keihin-tohoku Line
Keikyu Line
Keikyu Kuko Line

Keikyu-kamata
Tenkubashi

Hatsu-magome

Oedo Line
Namboku Line
Mita Line
Asakusa Line
Hanzomon Line
Ginza Line

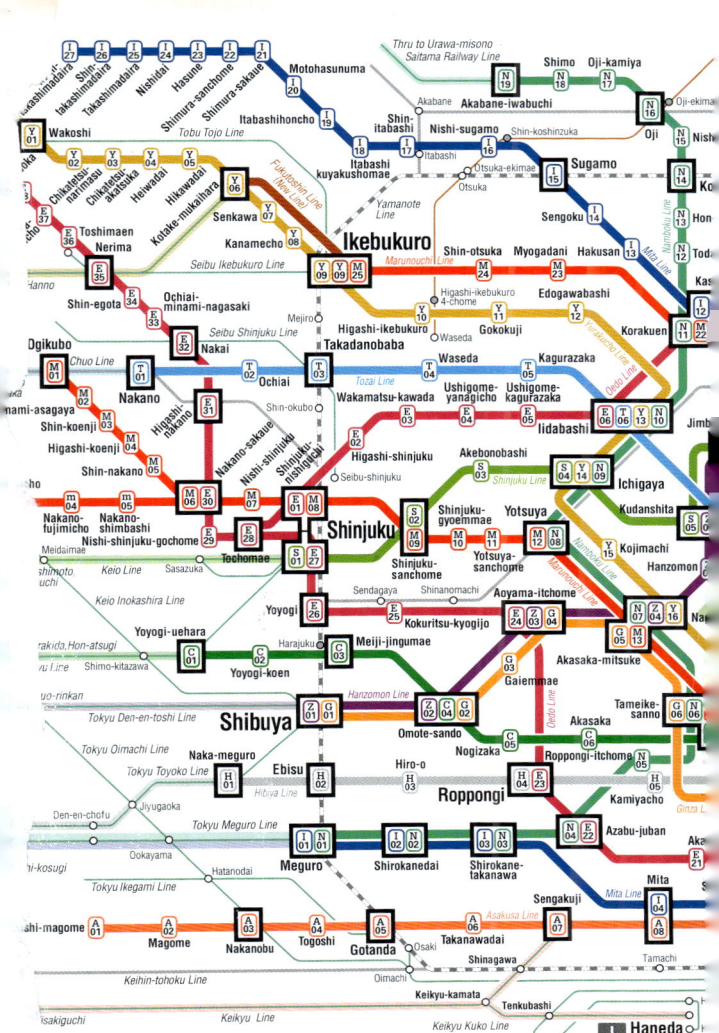

✈ Haneda Airport

THE LITTLE
TOKYO SUBWAY GUIDEBOOK

Tokyo Subway Route Map

BUREAU OF TRANSPORTATION
TOKYO METROPOLITAN GOVERNMENT

Line Color

Line Symbol

Station Number

Toei Line		Tokyo Metro Line	
A Asakusa Line		**G** Ginza Line	
I Mita Line		**Mm** Marunouchi Line	
S Shinjuku Line		**H** Hibiya Line	
E Oedo Line		**T** Tozai Line	
	Junctions	**C** Chiyoda Line	
	JR Yamanote Line	**Y** Yurakucho Line	
	JR Line	**F** Fukutoshin Line (New Line)	
	Private Railways	**Z** Hanzomon Line	
	Toei Streetcar Arakawa Line	**N** Namboku Line	

BUREAU OF TRANSPORTATION TOKYO METROPOLITAN GOVERNMENT   Tokyo Metro Co. Ltd. © 2006.3

THE LITTLE

TOKYO
SUBWAY
GUIDEBOOK

© 2007 IBC Publishing, Inc.

Published by IBC Publishing, Inc.
Akasaka Community Bldg. 5F, 1-1-8 Moto-Akasaka
Minato-ku, Tokyo 107-0051
www.ibcpub.co.jp

Distributed by Yohan, Inc.
Akasaka Community Bldg. 5/6/7F, 1-1-8 Moto-Akasaka
Minato-ku, Tokyo 107-0051

First edition 2007
Designed by Ryoichi Kawarada
ISBN978-4-89684-457-3
Printed in Japan

The contents of this book are based on the data and information at the time of publication,
and subject to change without notice.

Table of Contents

Landmark Finder: Find the Nearest Station 67

Information

Index of Stations

Introduction

Tokyo provides all kinds of public transportation, including buses, taxis, and water buses, but the fastest and most efficient way of getting through the heart of the city is the subway. Tokyo has a total of 13 subway lines that cover most of the major areas of the city. Some subway lines even make their way into the neighboring prefectures of Chiba, and Saitama. One major advantage of taking the subway is that you don't have to worry about the weather or traffic!

Nine of the subway lines are run by Tokyo Metro (privatized in 2004), and four are operated by the Tokyo Metropolitan Bureau of Transportation (Toei). The two systems require different tickets, which can make things a little confusing. A numbering system shared by both companies makes it easy to distinguish one station from another. The train lines are also indicated by different colors to make it easy for people who don't speak Japanese to get to their destination with ease.

This book gives you the lowdown on the Tokyo subway system and fully explains the all-important numbering system. Once you know the basics, getting around Tokyo is a cinch.

Here too you will find lots of other useful information about the subway system. Use the maps included here and get to your destination in a flash. Just slide the book into your pocket, grab your coat, and you're off!

The System:

How to Use the Subway

1. Spot the entrance to the subway.
2. Find out how much you have to pay.
3. Buy your ticket.
4. Go through the gate.
5. Go out the gate.
6. Find the exit.

1 Spot the entrance to the subway.

The following symbols are used to indicate the subway:

Subway

Tokyo Metro

Toei Subway

Asakusa Station,
Ginza Line

Find the line you want to ride using the Station Numbering System.

All Tokyo subway lines use a numbering system to designate stations. This means you can know where you are without being able to read Japanese (or English for that matter). The colored circle matches the color of the subway line. The letter (on the top) signifies the name of the train line, and the number below indicates the station on that line. As a rule the numbers rise (01, 02, 03) going from west to east or south to north.

Line Symbol + Line Color

Tokyo Metro

Ginza Line

Yurakucho Line (Y)

Marunouchi Line (M) or (m)

Fukutoshin Line (O)
(Open June 2008)

Hibiya Line (H)

Hanzomon Line (Z)

Tozai Line (T)

Namboku Line (N)

Chiyoda Line (C)

Toei Subway

Asakusa Line	**A**	Shinjuku Line	**S**
Mita Line	**I**	Oedo Line	**E**

2 Find out how much you have to pay.

Tickets for Toei Subway lines can only be used on Toei Subway lines, and tickets for Tokyo Metro lines can only be used on Tokyo Metro lines. There are transfer tickets available that save you money and can be used for both lines. Confirm the correct fare on the English fare chart next to the ticket vending machines.

3 Buy your ticket.

Put your money into the automatic ticket vending machine. Push the button for the correct fare to your destination. Take your ticket. Don't forget your change!

4 Go through the gate.

There are automatic ticket gates at every station. Put the ticket in the slot and then retrieve it when it pops out at the other end. (Do not try to insert your ticket if you see a red No Entry sign on the gate.) After you pass through the gate, follow the signs to the numbered platform where you will board your train. Hold on to your ticket until you reach your destination.

5 Go out the gate.

When you get to your destination station insert your ticket into the slot in the atomatic ticket gate and exit.
If you discover you've bought the wrong ticket, pay the additional fare before exiting using the adjustment machine located near the ticket gate. If you mistakenly paid more than the required fare, you cannot get a refund.

How to Use the Fare Adjustment Machine
Insert your ticket.
If you have transferred at a station, select the station you passed through.
Insert the amount of money shown on the screen.
An adjustment ticket is provided.
Use the adjustment ticket at the automatic ticket gate.

6 Find the exit.

Find the station exit closest to your destination on the station map (usually located on a large panel near the gate). Each station exit can be identified by a unique number and letter.

Tickets

Regular Ticket   (*Futsuken*)
Coupon Ticket   (*Kaisuken*)
Railway Pass   (*Teikiken*)
Pasmo
Special Ticket

Regular Ticket (*Futsuken*)

Regular Tickets are sold at every station. These tickets are only valid on the day you buy them. They become void once you exit the gate.The following are regular ticket fares for adult:

Tokyo Metro Regular Ticket

Tokyo Metro: ¥160, ¥190, ¥230, ¥270, ¥300
Toei Subway: ¥170, ¥210, ¥260, ¥310, ¥360, ¥410

The regular fare is based on the minimum distance between the stations where you begin and end your journey, regardless of the actual route you take.

Tokyo Metro Regular Fares by Distance

1 km – 6 km	¥160	(¥80 for children)
7 km – 11 km	¥190	(¥100 for children)
12 km – 19 km	¥230	(¥120 for children)
20 km – 27 km	¥270	(¥140 for children)
28 km – 40 km	¥300	(¥150 for children)

Toei Subway Regular Fares by Distance

1 km – 4 km	¥170	(¥90 for children)
5 km – 9 km	¥210	(¥110 for children)
10 km – 15 km	¥260	(¥130 for children)
16 km – 21 km	¥310	(¥160 for children)
22 km – 27 km	¥360	(¥180 for children)
28 km – 46 km	¥410	(¥210 for children)

Fares for Children are Half the Price of Adult Fares

Adult fare Adult = 12 or over (junior high and above)

Child fare Child = 6–11 years old (includes 12 year olds still in elementary school)

Toddler fare Toddler = 1–5 years old (includes 6 year olds not yet in school)*

Free Infant = under 1 year old

* Fare is free for up to two children if accompanied by an adult. Fare is required for three or more children. Children must pay if unaccompanied by an adult. Children's tickets are sold at automatic vending machines.

Transfer Ticket (Regular)

You will receive a discount on your fare if you use a transfer ticket to switch between Tokyo Metro lines and Toei Subway lines. You save ¥70 regardless of the actual route you take.

To buy a transfer ticket, push the transfer button on the ticket vending machine.

Coupon Ticket (*Kaisuken*)

11 tickets for the price of 10. Arrival and departure stations, date and time of use, are not specified. These are sold at automatic vending machines and pass offices at Tokyo Metro and Toei Subway stations. Each ticket is only valid for the line it is purchased for. The price of the coupon is equal to the fare

Tokyo Metro
Coupon ticket

for a particular zone times ten. If you travel further than the particular zone, you must pay the extra fare. It is valid for up to three months after purchase.

In addition, it is possible to purchase 12 tickets for the price of 10 for off-peak hours (Monday through Friday 10:00–16:00, Saturday, Sunday, holidays, and December 30–January 3) and 14 tickets for the price of 10 for holidays (Saturday, Sunday, holidays, and December 30–January 3).

Tokyo Metro Coupon Ticket Rates by Zone

¥160 zone	¥1, 600	(¥800 for children)
¥190 zone	¥1, 900	(¥1, 000 for children)
¥230 zone	¥2, 300	(¥1, 200 for children)
¥270 zone	¥2, 700	(¥1, 400 for children)
¥300 zone	¥3, 000	(¥1, 500 for children)

Toei Subway Coupon Ticket Rates by Zone

¥170 zone	¥1, 700	(¥900 for children)
¥210 zone	¥2, 100	(¥1, 100 for children)
¥260 zone	¥2, 600	(¥1, 300 for children)
¥310 zone	¥3, 100	(¥1, 600 for children)
¥360 zone	¥3, 600	(¥1, 800 for children)
¥410 zone	¥4, 100	(¥2, 100 for children)

Railway Pass (*Teikiken*)

You can buy railway passes for commuting to work or school, for which you register and determine the line and zone you want to use. There are also "all line" passes (zensen teikiken) that can be used for all Tokyo Metro lines or all Toei lines. These passes are valid for one, three, or six months. The zensen passes can be used by any person carrying the pass, as long as it is within the period of validity.

PASMO

PASMO is a rechargeable smart card that lets you travel on subways, on both private and JR trains, and on buses within metro Tokyo without having to buy a separate ticket for each ride. Just touch the PASMO to the card reader at the ticket gate and the amount of the fare is automatically computed and deducted. As long as the fare required is less than the amount charged on the card you can ride and transfer without having to wait in line or hunt for change at a ticket machine.

PASMO cards can be bought at participating stations and bus depots in units of ¥1,000 yen up to ¥20,000 (the first ¥500 is a deposit against loss and is refunded to you when you no longer need the card).

Special Tickets

Several special tickets are available that can be matched to your particular needs to save you money.

Tokyo Free Ticket

Unlimited use of Tokyo Metro, Toei Subways, Toei Streetcars, Toei Buses (except when seats are limited), and/or JR East lines within the Tokyo wards for one day.

Adult: ¥1, 580   Child: ¥790

Sales Locations: Pass offices at Tokyo Metro stations (excluding Nishi-funabashi Station), Toei Streetcars/Buses offices, Toei Subway stations and pass offices, JR stations in Tokyo wards).
Period of Validity: 6 months after the date of purchase.
Area of Validity: Tokyo Metro, Toei Subway, Toei Streetcars, Toei Buses (except late-night buses and limited-seating buses), JR in Tokyo.
Refund: Availabe only for unused tickets that have not expired. A ¥210 fee will be charged.

Tokyo Metro and Toei Subway Common One-Day Economy Pass

Unlimited use of Tokyo Metro and Toei Subway lines for one day.

Adult: ¥1, 000   Child: ¥500

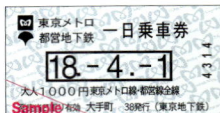

Sales Locations: Vending machines at Tokyo Metro stations and Toei Subway stations.
Period of Validity: Day of purchase.
Area of Validity: All Tokyo Metro lines, all Toei Subway lines.
Refund: Available only for unused passes that have not expired. A ¥210 fee will be charged.

Tokyo Metro One-Day Open Ticket

Good for unlimited use for one day on Tokyo Metro lines only. It can be purchased on day-of-use or in advance.

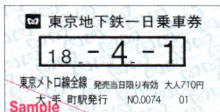

Day-of-use Ticket
(for adult)

Advance Ticket
(for adult)

Adult: ¥710   Child: ¥360

Sales Locations: Advance tickets are sold at pass office (excluding Nakano, Nishi-funabashi stations), and day-of-use tickets are sold at vending machines at Tokyo Metro stations.

Period of Validity: Advance tickets are valid up to six months from day of purchase; day-of-use tickets are valid only on day of purchase.

Area of Validity: All Tokyo Metro lines.

Refund: Available only for unused passes that have not expired. A ¥210 fee will be charged.

Toei Streetcar, Bus and Subway One-Day Economy Pass

Unlimited use of Toei streetcars, buses, and subways within 23 wards of Tokyo (including Tama district) for one day. (An additional ¥200 is required for late-night buses.)

Adult: ¥700   Child: ¥350

Sales Locations: Advance passes are available at station counters for Toei Subway stations, Toei Streetcar/Bus offices, Arakawa Train Office, Toei Streetcar/Bus pass offices. For day-of-use passes, use automatic vending machines at Toei Subway stations or purchase directly on streetcars or buses. (Day-of-use passes are also available where advance passes are sold.)

Period of Validity: Advance tickets are valid up to six months from day of purchase; day-of-use tickets are valid only on day of purchase.

Limousine and Metro Pass Ticket

Ticket set including one-way travel on limousine buses from/to Narita International Airport (Narita Airport) or Tokyo International Airport (Haneda Airport) to/from various locations within Tokyo, and also unlimited usage of all Tokyo Metro lines for one day.

ex.) Narita Airport ⇔ Tokyo, Shinjuku, Major Tokyo Hotels

Adults: ¥3,100   Children: ¥1,550

ex.) Haneda Airport ⇔ Akasaka, Kudan, Korakuen

Adults: ¥1,400   Children: ¥700

Sales Locations: Limousine Bus Counter at Narita Airport (for buses departing from Narita Airport) and Haneda Airport Information Counter (for buses departing from Haneda Airport), Tokyo City Air Terminal (T-CAT), Limousine Bus Ticket Counter at Shinjuku Station, and pass offices for Tokyo Metro stations (excluding Nakano and Nishi-funabashi stations.)

Period of Validity: limousine bus. One time within six months of purchase.

Tokyo Metro. One day within six months of purchase. (The limousine bus ticket and Tokyo Metro tickets can be used on separate days.)

Area of Validity: Limousine bus. One way to/from Narita Airport or Haneda Airport on routes within Tokyo.

Tokyo Metro. All Tokyo Metro lines.

Transfer:
Find Your Route

Ginza Line	Oedo Line
Marunouchi Line	JR Yamanote Line
Hibiya Line	JR Chuo Line
Tozai Line	Yokohama-shiei Subway and Minatomirai Line
Chiyoda Line	
Yurakucho Line	
Hanzomon Line	
Namboku Line	
Asakusa Line	
Mita Line	
Shinjuku Line	

- ▦ Public Offices
- Theaters, Stadiums, Auditoriums
- F Museums
- Places of Worship
- Parks, Gardens, Zoos
- Shopping Streets
- Hotels

❶ Station Name
❷ Line Symbol and Station Code
❸ Express Stop
❹ Local Stop
❺ Time Between Stations
❻ Time from First Station
❼ Transfer Lines
❽ Transfer Station
❾ Interoperating Line

Keio Line

Shinjuku 新宿
S 01
● Oedo Line
● JR Line
○ Odakyu Line
○ Keio Line

Bakuroyokoyama 馬喰横山
S 09
● Asakusa Line (A15)
● JR Line

Hamacho 浜町
S 10

Ginza LINE

The Ginza Line was the first subway line ever built in Asia. It was opened on December 30, 1927, and ran from Asakusa to Ueno (not a very great distance). During the 20's and 30's, two separate lines stretched from Asakusa to Shimbashi, and Shimbashi to Shibuya. In 1939 the two lines were connected at Shimbashi to form one line. The subway line was subsequently handed over to the Teito Rapid Transit Authority(TRTA) in 1941. In 1953, the line was officially named the "Ginza Line" after the trendiest city district in Japan at the time.

Station	Line(s)	min
G 01 Shibuya 渋谷	Hanzomon Line; Fukutoshin Line (Open June 2008)	
G 02 Omote-sando 表参道	JR Line; Tokyu Toyoko Line; Tokyu Den-en-toshi Line; Keio Inokashira Line; Chiyoda Line; Hanzomon Line	2 min / 2 min / 2 / 4
G 03 Gaiemmae 外苑前		1 / 5
G 04 Aoyama-itchome 青山一丁目	Hanzomon Line; Oedo Line	2 / 7
G 05 Akasaka-mitsuke 赤坂見附	Marunouchi Line; Yurakucho Line (Y16); Hanzomon Line (Z04); Namboku Line (N07)	2 / 9
G 06 Tameike-sanno 溜池山王	Namboku Line; Marunouchi Line (M14); Chiyoda Line (C07)	2 / 11
G 07 Toranomon 虎ノ門		2 / 13
G 08 Shimbashi 新橋	Asakusa Line; JR Line; Yurikamome Line	2 / 15
G 09 Ginza 銀座	Marunouchi Line; Hibiya Line	2 / 17
G 10 Kyobashi 京橋		

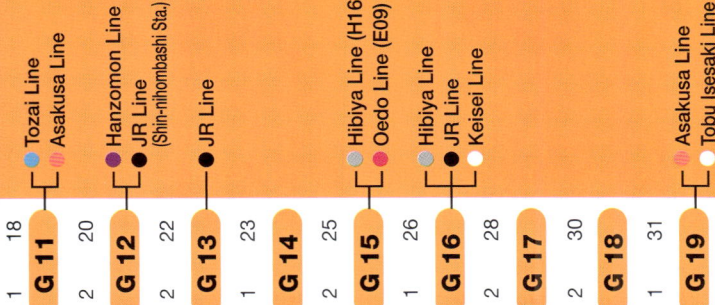

Marunouchi LINE

The Marunouchi Line was the first train line built by the TRTA. Construction began in 1942 but was temporarily halted by the Second World War. Work on the line resumed in 1951. Starting from Ikebukuro, it passes through business areas like Marunouchi (for which it is named), Yotsuya, and Shinjuku. Part of the line branches off from Nakano-sakaue toward Honancho west of Shinjuku.

Station	Code		
Ogikubo 荻窪	**M 01**	2min	2min
Minami-asagaya 南阿佐ケ谷	**M 02**	2	4
Shin-koenji 新高円寺	**M 03**	2	6
Higashi-koenji 東高円寺	**M 04**	2	8
Shin-nakano 新中野	**M 05**	2	10
Nakano-sakaue 中野坂上	**M 06**	2	12
Nishi-shinjuku 西新宿	**M 07**	2	14
Shinjuku 新宿	**M 08**	1	15
Shinjuku-sanchome 新宿三丁目	**M 09**	2	17
Shinjuku-gyoemmae 新宿御苑前	**M 10**	2	19

Oedo Line

Shinjuku Line
Oedo Line (E01)
JR Line
Odakyu Line
Keio Line
Seibu Shinjuku Line

Shinjuku Line
Fukutoshin Line
(Open June 2008)

Station	Code		
Nakano-shimbashi 中野新橋	**m 05**	2	4
Nakano-fujimicho 中野富士見町	**m 04**	2	2
Honancho 方南町	**m 03**	2	0

Marunouchi Line (M)

Station	No.	Connecting Lines
M 11	2 21	**Yotsuya-sanchome** 四谷三丁目
M 12	2 23	**Yotsuya** 四ツ谷 — Namboku Line / JR Line
M 13	3 26	**Akasaka-mitsuke** 赤坂見附 — Ginza Line / Yurakucho Line (Y16)
M 14	2 28	**Kokkai-gijidomae** 国会議事堂前 — Hanzomon Line (Z04) / Namboku Line (N07) / Chiyoda Line / Ginza Line (G06) / Namboku Line (N06)
M 15	2 30	**Kasumigaseki** 霞ヶ関 — Hibiya Line / Chiyoda Line
M 16	2 32	**Ginza** 銀座 — Ginza Line / Hibiya Line
M 17	2 34	**Tokyo** 東京 — JR Line
M 18	2 36	**Otemachi** 大手町 — Tozai Line / Chiyoda Line / Hanzomon Line / Mita Line
M 19	1 37	**Awajicho** 淡路町 — Chiyoda Line (C12) / Shinjuku Line (S07)
M 20	2 39	**Ochanomizu** 御茶ノ水 — JR Line

Station	No.	Connecting Lines
M 25	3 48	**Ikebukuro** 池袋 — Yurakucho Line / Fukutoshin Line (Open June 2008) / JR Line / Seibu Ikebukuro Line / Tobu Tojo Line
M 24	2 45	**Shin-otsuka** 新大塚
M 23	2 43	**Myogadani** 茗荷谷
M 22	2 41	**Korakuen** 後楽園 — Namboku Line / Mita Line (I12) / Oedo Line (E07)
M 21	2	**Hongo-sanchome** 本郷三丁目 — Oedo Line

Hibiya LINE

The opening of the Hibiya Line was timed to coincide with the Tokyo Olympics of 1964. It runs from Kita-senju in the northeast to Naka-meguro in the southwest, passing through Ueno, Ginza, Kasumigaseki, Roppongi, and other areas. It also interoperates with the Tobu Isesaki Line (part of which is the Nikko Line) from Kita-senju Station, and the Tokyu Toyoko Line from Naka-meguro Station. The name comes from the Hibiya area, through which the line passes.

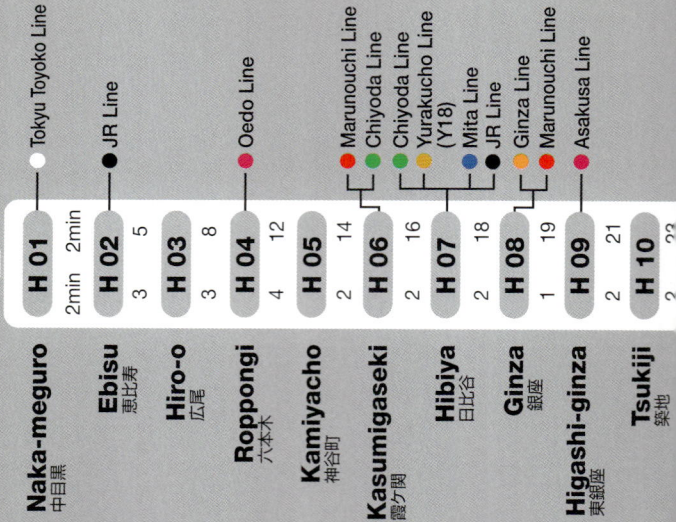

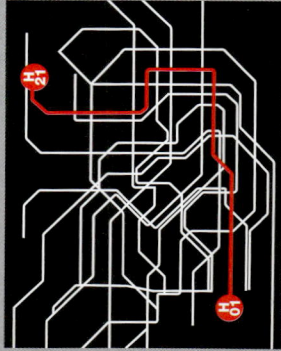

Station	Code		Connections
Naka-meguro 中目黒	H 01		Tokyu Toyoko Line
		2min 2min	
Ebisu 恵比寿	H 02		JR Line
		3 5	
Hiro-o 広尾	H 03		
		3 8	
Roppongi 六本木	H 04		Oedo Line
		4 12	
Kamiyacho 神谷町	H 05		
		2 14	
Kasumigaseki 霞ヶ関	H 06		Marunouchi Line / Chiyoda Line
		2 16	
Hibiya 日比谷	H 07		Chiyoda Line / Yurakucho Line (Y18) / Mita Line / JR Line
		2 18	
Ginza 銀座	H 08		Ginza Line / Marunouchi Line
		1 19	
Higashi-ginza 東銀座	H 09		Asakusa Line
		2 21	
Tsukiji 築地	H 10		

24

Tokyo Metro Hibiya Line

Station			Connecting Lines
H 11	2	25	JR Line
H 12	2	27	Tozai Line
H 13	2	29	Asakusa Line
H 14	2	31	JR Line
H 15	1	32	Tsukuba Express Line · Ginza Line (G15) · Oedo Line (E09) · JR Line (Okachimachi Sta.)
H 16	2	34	Tsukuba Express Line · Ginza Line (G15) · Oedo Line (E09) · JR Line (Okachimachi Sta.)
H 17	2	36	Ginza Line
H 18	2	38	JR Line · Keisei Line
H 19	2	40	JR Line · Tsukuba Express Line
H 20	3	43	Chiyoda Line · JR Line · Tobu Isesaki Line · Tsukuba Express Line
H 21			Chiyoda Line · JR Line · Tobu Isesaki Line · Tsukuba Express Line

Tobu Isesaki Line

- **Hatchobori** 八丁堀 (H 11)
- **Kayabacho** 茅場町 (H 12)
- **Ningyocho** 人形町 (H 13)
- **Kodemmacho** 小伝馬町 (H 14)
- **Akihabara** 秋葉原 (H 15)
- **Naka-okachimachi** 仲御徒町 (H 16)
- **Ueno** 上野 (H 17)
- **Iriya** 入谷 (H 18)
- **Minowa** 三ノ輪 (H 19)
- **Minami-senju** 南千住 (H 20)
- **Kita-senju** 北千住 (H 21)

H-02	Westin Tokyo
H-04	Mori Art Museum
H-04	National Art Center, Tokyo
H-04	Roppongi Hills
H-04	Tokyo Midtown
H-05	Tokyo Tower/Shiba Park
H-07	Hibiya Park
H-07	Imperial Hotel
H-07	Imperial Palace/Nijubashi
H-07	Tokyo Takarazuka Theater
H-09	Kabuki-za Theater
H-10	Tsukiji Honganji Temple
H-10	Tsukiji Market
H-13	Suitengu Shrine
H-15	Akihabara Electric City
H-17	Kan-eiji Temple
H-17	National Science Museum, Tokyo
H-17	Tokyo Metropolitan Art Museum
H-17	Tokyo National Museum
H-17	Toshogu Shrine
H-17	Ueno Onshi Park (Shinobazunoike Pond)
H-17	Ueno Royal Museum
H-17	Ueno Zoo

Tozai LINE

"Tozai" means "east and west" in Japanese. The Tozai Line starts in the east at Nishi-funabashi in Chiba Prefecture and goes west to Nakano in Tokyo. It interoperates with the JR Sobu Line and Toyo Rapid Line from Nishi-funabashi, and the JR Chuo Line from Nakano. The Tozai Line has the longest operation distance among the Tokyo Metro lines, and even though it is a subway over one-third of it runs above ground. It is also the only Tokyo Metro line that has an express train.

JR Chuo Line

Station		Time	Cumulative	Connections
T 01	Nakano 中野	3min	3min	JR Line
T 02	Ochiai 落合	3	6	
T 03	Takadanobaba 高田馬場	3	9	JR Line, Seibu Shinjuku Line
T 04	Waseda 早稲田	2	11	
T 05	Kagurazaka 神楽坂	2	13	Yurakucho Line, Namboku Line, Oedo Line
T 06	Iidabashi 飯田橋	2	15	JR Line
T 07	Kudanshita 九段下	2	17	Hanzomon Line, Shinjuku Line
T 08	Takebashi 竹橋	3	20	
T 09	Otemachi 大手町	1	21	Marunouchi Line, Chiyoda Line, Hanzomon Line, Mita Line
T 10	Nihombashi 日本橋	2	23	Ginza Line, Asakusa Line
T 11	Kayabacho 茅場町	2	25	Hibiya Line

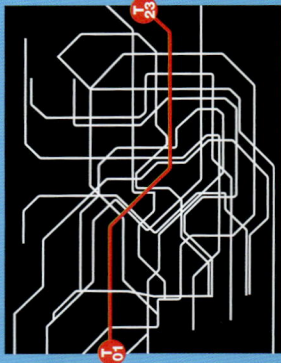

Monzen-nakacho 門前仲町	**T 12**	2	27
Kiba 木場	**T 13**	1	28
Toyocho 東陽町	**T 14**	3	31
Minami-sunamachi 南砂町	**T 15**	3	34
Nishi-kasai 西葛西	**T 16**	3	36
Kasai 葛西	**T 17**	2	38
Urayasu 浦安	**T 18**	2	40
Minami-gyotoku 南行徳	**T 19**	2	42
Gyotoku 行徳	**T 20**	2	44
Myoden 妙典	**T 21**	2	47
Baraki-nakayama 原木中山	**T 22**	3	47
Nishi-funabashi 西船橋	**T 23**	3	50

● Oedo Line

● JR Line
○ Toyo Rapid Line

Toyo Rapid Line
JR Sobu Line

T-01 Nakano Sunplaza [A]
T-03 Big Box [A]
T-04 International Medical Center of Japan
T-04 Ringa Royal Hotel Tokyo [icon]
T-04 Waseda University
T-06 Hotel Metropolitan Edmont [icon]
T-07 Kudan Kaikan [icon]
T-07 Nippon Budokan [icon]
T-07 Yasukuni Jinja Shrine [icon]
T-08 Japan Meteorological Agency [icon]
T-08 National Museum of Modern Art [F]
T-08 Science Museum [F]
T-09 Imperial Palace Higashi-gyoen [F]
T-09 Palace Hotel Tokyo [icon]
T-10 Coredo Nihombashi [icon]
T-10 Nihombashi Bridge
T-10 Nihombashi Takashimaya [A]
T-12 Kiyosumi Garden [F]
T-12 Tomioka Hachimangu Shrine [icon]
T-13 Kiba Park [F]
T-17 Subway Museum [F]
T-17 Tokyo Sea Life Park [F]
T-18 Urayasu Fish Market [A]

Chiyoda LINE

The Chiyoda Line was originally constructed as a bypass to the crowded Hibiya Line. It runs from the northeast to the southwest, by the imperial palace and central government headquarters as well as through Chiyoda Ward (for which it is named), where many company headquarters are located. In the northeast, it interoperates with the JR Joban Line from Ayase and also branches off toward Kita-ayase. In the southwest, it interoperates with the Odakyu Odawara Line and the Tama Line from Yoyogi-uehara.

Odakyu Odawara Line
Odakyu Tama Line

Station	Time	Connecting Lines
C 01 Yoyogi-uehara 代々木上原		Odakyu Line
C 02 Yoyogi-koen 代々木公園	2min / 2min	
C 03 Meiji-jingumae 明治神宮前	2 / 4	Fukutoshin Line (Open June 2008); JR Line
C 04 Omote-sando 表参道	1 / 5	Ginza Line; Hanzomon Line
C 05 Nogizaka 乃木坂	3 / 8	
C 06 Akasaka 赤坂	2 / 10	
C 07 Kokkai-gijidomae 国会議事堂前	1 / 11	Marunouchi Line; Ginza Line(G06); Namboku Line(N06)
C 08 Kasumigaseki 霞ケ関	2 / 13	Marunouchi Line; Hibiya Line
C 09 Hibiya 日比谷	2 / 15	Hibiya Line; Yurakucho Line (Y18)
C 10 Nijubashimae 二重橋前	2 / 17	Mita Line; JR Line
	1 / 18	

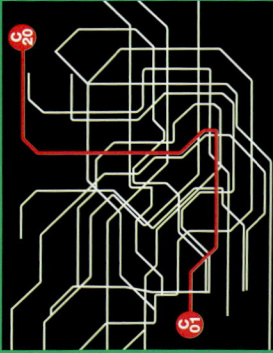

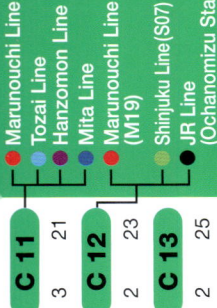

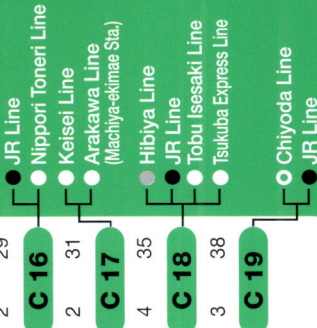

Station	Name		
Connections	Marunouchi Line · Tozai Line · Hanzomon Line · Mita Line · Marunouchi Line (M19) · Shinjuku Line (S07) · JR Line (Ochanomizu Sta.)		
C 11	**Otemachi** 大手町	3	21
C 12	**Shin-ochanomizu** 新御茶ノ水	2	23
C 13	**Yushima** 湯島	2	25
C 14	**Nezu** 根津	2	27
C 15	**Sendagi** 千駄木	2	29
C 16	**Nishi-nippori** 西日暮里 (JR Line · Nippori Toneri Line)	2	31
C 17	**Machiya** 町屋 (Keisei Line · Arakawa Line (Machiya-ekimae Sta.))	4	35
C 18	**Kita-senju** 北千住 (Hibiya Line · JR Line · Tobu Isesaki Line · Tsukuba Express Line)	3	38
C 19	**Ayase** 綾瀬 (Chiyoda Line · JR Line)	4	4
C 20	**Kita-ayase** 北綾瀬	4	4

JR Joban Line ▶

Yurakucho LINE

From Wakoshi in Saitama Prefecture, the Yurakucho Line cuts across Tokyo from the northwest to southeast, going through Kotake-mukaihara, Ikebukuro, and Nagatacho. It ends in Shinkiba. From Wakoshi, it interoperates with the Tobu Tojo Line, and from Kotake-mukaihara it interoperates with the Seibu Ikebukuro Line by way of the Seibu Yurakucho Line. The Fukutoshin Line, scheduled to open in June 2008, will run from Wakoshi, Saitama Prefecture, to Ikebukuro, and then past Shinjuku to Shibuya.

Fukutoshin Line (Open June 2008)

Tobu Tojo Line

Seibu Yurakucho Line

Y 01	3min	Wakoshi 和光市
	3min	
Y 02	2	Chikatetsu-narimasu 地下鉄成増
	5	
Y 03	3	Chikatetsu-akatsuka 地下鉄赤塚
	8	
Y 04	2	Heiwadai 平和台
	10	
Y 05	2	Hikawadai 氷川台
	12	
Y 06	2	Kotake-mukaihara 小竹向原
	14	
Y 07	2	Senkawa 千川
	16	
Y 08	2	Kanamecho 要町
	18	
Y 09	3	Ikebukuro 池袋
	21	
Y 10		Higashi-ikebukuro 東池袋
	23	

Shibuya 渋谷
Meiji-jingumae 明治神宮前
Kita-sando 北参道
Shinjuku-sanchome 新宿三丁目
Shinjuku 新宿
Higashi-shinjuku 東新宿
Nishi-waseda 西早稲田
Zoshigaya 雑司が谷

● Marunouchi Line
● JR Line
○ Tobu Tojo Line
○ Seibu Ikebukuro Line
○ Arakawa Line (Higashi-ikebukuro-yonchome Sta.)

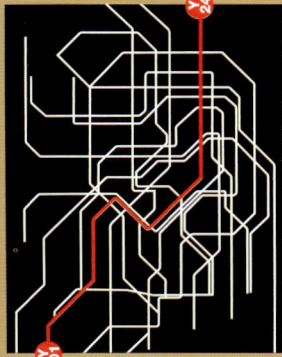

Station	Number		Transfer Lines
Y11	25	2	Gokokuji 護国寺
Y12	28	3	Edogawabashi 江戸川橋
Y13	30	2	Iidabashi 飯田橋 — Tozai Line / Namboku Line / Oedo Line / JR Line
Y14	32	2	Ichigaya 市ヶ谷 — Namboku Line / Shinjuku Line / JR Line
Y15	34	2	Kojimachi 麹町
Y16	36	2	Nagatacho 永田町 — Hanzomon Line / Namboku Line / Ginza Line (G05) / Marunouchi Line (M13)
Y17	37	1	Sakuradamon 桜田門
Y18	39	2	Yurakucho 有楽町 — Hibiya Line (H07) / Chiyoda Line (C09) / Mita Line (I08) / JR Line
Y19	41	2	Ginza-itchome 銀座一丁目
Y20	43	2	Shintomicho 新富町
Y21			Tsukishima 月島 — Oedo Line
Y22	45	2	Toyosu 豊洲 — Yurikamome Line
Y23	47	2	Tatsumi 辰巳
Y24	50	3	Shin-kiba 新木場 — JR Line / Rinkai Line

Hanzomon LINE

The Hanzomon Line runs from Shibuya to Nagatacho, rounds the northern part of the imperial palace, passes through Otemachi, and ends in Oshiage. It interoperates with the Tokyu Den-en-toshi Line from Shibuya and with the Tobu Isesaki Line and the Nikko Line from Oshiage. "Hanzomon" refers to a gate in the imperial palace near the residence of Hattori Hanzo, a retainer of the first Shogun of the Edo period, Tokugawa Ieyasu.

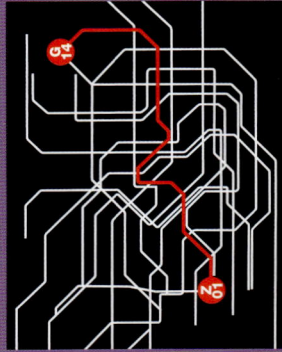

Station	Code			Lines
Shibuya 渋谷	Z 01	2min	2min	Ginza Line / Fukutoshin Line (Open June 2008) / JR Line / Tokyu Toyoko Line / Tokyu Den-en-toshi Line / Keio Inokashira Line
Omote-sando 表参道	Z 02	2	4	Ginza Line / Chiyoda Line
Aoyama-itchome 青山一丁目	Z 03		7	Ginza Line / Oedo Line
Nagatacho 永田町	Z 04	3		Yurakucho Line / Namboku Line / Ginza Line (G05) / Marunouchi Line (M13)
Hanzomon 半蔵門	Z 05	2	9	
Kudanshita 九段下	Z 06	2	11	Tozai Line / Shinjuku Line
Jimbocho 神保町	Z 07	1	12	Mita Line / Shinjuku Line
		3	15	

Marunouchi Line
Tozai Line
Chiyoda Line
Mita Line

Ginza Line
JR Line
(Shin-nihombashi Sta.)

Oedo Line

Shinjuku Line

JR Line

Asakusa Line
Tobu Isesaki Line
Keisei Oshiage Line

Z 08		Z 09		Z 10		Z 11		Z 12		Z 13		Z 14
	17		20		23		26		28		30	
2		3		3		3		2		2		

Otemachi
大手町

Mitsukoshimae
三越前

Suitengumae
水天宮前

Kiyosumi-shirakawa
清澄白河

Sumiyoshi
住吉

Kinshicho
錦糸町

Oshiage
押上

Tobu Isesaki Line

Z-01	Bunkamura
Z-01	Hachiko-mae Square
Z-01	Shibuya Center Town
Z-01	SHIBUYA109
Z-01	Tokyu Hands Shibuya
Z-02	Aoyama Gakuin University
Z-02	Laforet Harajuku
Z-02	Meiji Jingu Shrine Omotesando
Z-02	National Children's Castle
	(Aoyama Theater)
Z-02	Omotesando Hills
Z-02	Taro Okamoto Memorial Museum
Z-02	Tokyo Women's Plaza
Z-02	United Nations University
Z-03	Meiji Jingu Shrine Outer Gardens
Z-04	Akasaka Prince Hotel
Z-04	Hotel New Otani
Z-05	National Theater
Z-06	Kudan Kaikan
Z-06	Nippon Budokan
Z-07	Kanda Secondhand Book Town
Z-08	Palace Hotel Tokyo
Z-09	Mandarin Oriental
Z-10	Suitengu Shrine
Z-11	Museum of Contemporary Art Tokyo

Namboku LINE

"Namboku" means "north and south" in Japanese, and the Namboku Line runs in exactly that direction. From Meguro in the south it interoperates with the Tokyu Meguro Line, and from Akabane Iwabuchi in the north it interoperates with the Saitama Railway Line. All its trains run by Automatic Train Operation (ATO), meaning that there is only one driver (most trains have one driver and one conductor). There are barriers installed on all the platforms, making this line a particularly safe one.

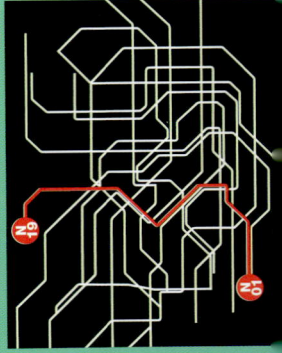

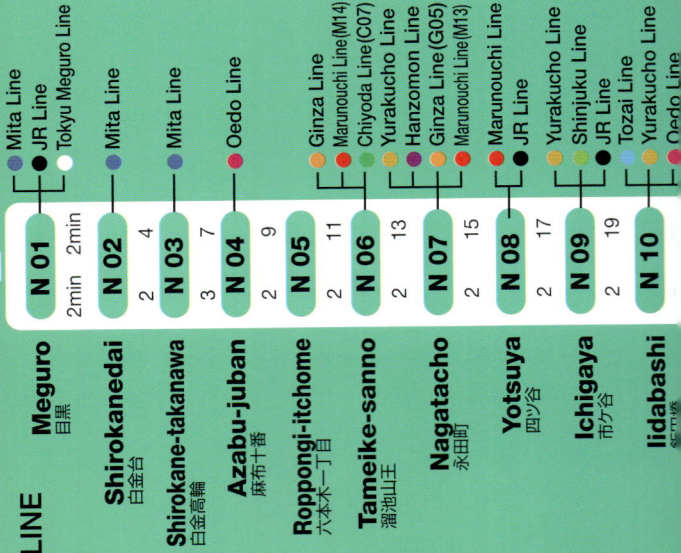

Station		Connections
Meguro 目黒	N 01	Mita Line / JR Line / Tokyu Meguro Line
	2min 2min	
Shirokanedai 白金台	N 02	Mita Line
	2 4	
Shirokane-takanawa 白金高輪	N 03	Mita Line
	3 7	
Azabu-juban 麻布十番	N 04	Oedo Line
	2 9	
Roppongi-itchome 六本木一丁目	N 05	Ginza Line / Marunouchi Line(M14)
	2 11	
Tameike-sanno 溜池山王	N 06	Chiyoda Line(C07) / Yurakucho Line
	2 13	
Nagatacho 永田町	N 07	Hanzomon Line / Ginza Line (G05) / Marunouchi Line(M13)
	2 15	
Yotsuya 四ツ谷	N 08	Marunouchi Line / JR Line
	2 17	
Ichigaya 市ケ谷	N 09	Yurakucho Line / Shinjuku Line / JR Line
	2 19	
Iidabashi 飯田橋	N 10	Tozai Line / Yurakucho Line / Oedo Line

Rail lines

- JR Line
- Marunouchi Line
- Mita Line (I12)
- Oedo Line (E07)
- JR Line
- JR Line
- Arakawa Line (Oji-ekimae Sta.)
- Saitama Railway Line

Stations

No.	Station		Transfers
N 11	Korakuen	後楽園	2 / 21
N 12	Todaimae	東大前	3 / 24
N 13	Hon-komagome	本駒込	2 / 26
N 14	Komagome	駒込	2 / 28
N 15	Nishigahara	西ヶ原	2 / 30
N 16	Oji	王子	2 / 32
N 17	Oji-kamiya	王子神谷	3 / 35
N 18	Shimo	志茂	2 / 37
N 19	Akabane-iwabuchi	赤羽岩淵	2 / 39

Saitama Railway Line

Facilities

Code	Facility
N-01	Megurogajo-en Garden
N-02	Happo-en Garden
N-02	Radisson Miyako Hotel Tokyo
N-02	Tokyo Metropolitan Teien Art Museum
N-04	Azabu Juban Shopping Town
N-05	Laforet Museum Harajuku
N-05	Suntory Hall
N-06	ANA Hotel Tokyo
N-06	Hie Jinja Shrine
N-06	Japan Patent Office
N-06	National Diet Building
N-07	Akasaka Prince Hotel
N-07	National Theater
N-07	Supreme Court of Japan
N-07/08	Hotel New Otani
N-08	Sophia University
N-08	State Guest House
N-09	Sotobori Park
N-11	Koishikawa Koraku-en Garden
N-11	Tokyo Dome City
N-14	Rikugi-en Garden
N-15	Kyu-Furukawa Teien Garden
N-16	Asukayama Park

Asakusa LINE

The Asakusa Line used to run from Asakusa to Oshiage; it was Toei Subway's first line and was simply called "Subway Line Ichi-go (Number 1)" from December 4, 1960 to 1978. The line now starts in Nishi-magome, passes through Nihom-bashi in the center of Tokyo, and runs all the way to Asakusa, for which it is now named (a downtown or "Shitamachi" district that maintains its "old Tokyo" feel). It interoperates with the Keisei Line and Hokuso Line from Oshiage and with the Keisei Line from Sengakuji Station.

■ LTD Express

Station	Code	Connections
Nishi-magome 西馬込	A 01	2min 2min
Magome 馬込	A 02	1　3
Nakanobu 中延	A 03	Tokyu Oimachi Line　2　5
Togoshi 戸越	A 04	2　7
Gotanda 五反田	A 05	JR Line / Tokyu Ikegami Line　2　9
Takanawadai 高輪台	A 06	2　11
Sengakuji 泉岳寺	A 07	Keikyu Line　2　13　2
Mita 三田	A 08	Mita Line　3　16　2
Daimon 大門	A 09	Oedo Line / JR Line / Tokyo Monorail　2　18　2
Shimbashi 新橋	A 10	Ginza Line / JR Line / Yurikamome Line　2

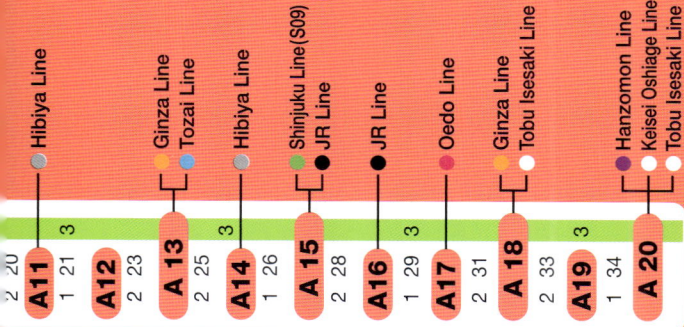

| | Hibiya Line | | Ginza Line / Tozai Line | Hibiya Line | Shinjuku Line (S09) / JR Line | JR Line | Oedo Line | Ginza Line / Tobu Isesaki Line | | Hanzomon Line / Keisei Oshiage Line / Tobu Isesaki Line |

A11 Higashi-ginza 東銀座 — 2 20, 1 21, 3
A12 Takaracho 宝町 — 2 23, 3
A13 Nihombashi 日本橋 — 2 25
A14 Ningyocho 人形町 — 1 26, 3
A15 Higashi-nihombashi 東日本橋 — 2 28
A16 Asakusabashi 浅草橋 — 1 29, 3
A17 Kuramae 蔵前 — 2 31
A18 Asakusa 浅草 — 2 33, 3
A19 Honjo-azumabashi 本所吾妻橋 — 1 34
A20 Oshiage 押上

Keisei Oshiage Line

A-06	Takanawa Prince Hotel
A-09	Kyu-Shibarikyu Onshi Teien Garden
A-09	Tokyo Prince Hotel
A-09	Tokyo Tower/Shiba Park
A-09	Zojoji Temple
A-11	Kabuki-za Theater
A-14	Suitengu Shrine
A-18	Asakusa Bunka Kanko Center
A-18	Asakusa Entertainment Hall
A-18	Asakusa Hanayashiki Amusement Park
A-18	Asakusa Kokaido
A-18	Azumabashi Bridge
A-18	Demboin Temple
A-18	Kaminarimon
A-18	Komagatabashi Bridge
A-18	Kototoibashi Bridge
A-18	Nakamise Dori
A-18	Sensoji Temple
A-18	Sumida Park
A-18	Sumidagawa River
A-18	Tokyo Water Cruise Asakusa Terminal

Mita LINE

The Mita Line starts in Nishi-takashimadaira, passes through the business areas of Otemachi Station and Uchisaiwai-cho, and travels on to Meguro Station, where it interoperates with the Tokyu Meguro Line. It is called the Mita Line, because Mita Station was the last stop when the line was first opened. There are safety barriers on the platforms of all the stations.

Tokyu Meguro Line

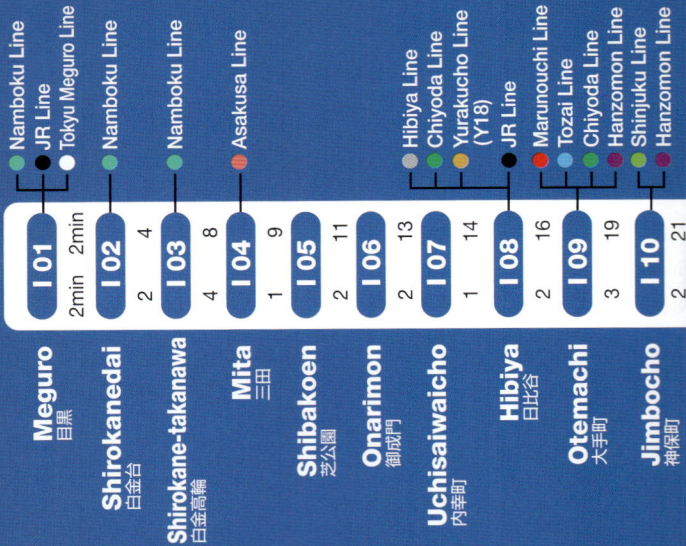

Station	Code	Time	Lines
Meguro 目黒	I 01	2min 2min	Namboku Line / JR Line / Tokyu Meguro Line
Shirokanedai 白金台	I 02	2 4	Namboku Line
Shirokane-takanawa 白金高輪	I 03	4 8	Namboku Line
Mita 三田	I 04	1 9	Asakusa Line
Shibakoen 芝公園	I 05	2 11	
Onarimon 御成門	I 06	2 13	
Uchisaiwaicho 内幸町	I 07	1 14	Hibiya Line / Chiyoda Line / Yurakucho Line (Y18)
Hibiya 日比谷	I 08	2 16	JR Line
Otemachi 大手町	I 09	3 19	Marunouchi Line / Tozai Line / Chiyoda Line / Hanzomon Line
Jimbocho 神保町	I 10	2 21	Shinjuku Line / Hanzomon Line

Legend

- ● JR Line
- ● Oedo Line
- ● Marunouchi Line (M22)
- ● Namboku Line (N11)
- ● JR Line
- ○ Arakawa Line

Station	Code	No.
Suidobashi 水道橋	I 11	2 · 23
Kasuga 春日	I 12	2 · 25
Hakusan 白山	I 13	2 · 27
Sengoku 千石	I 14	2 · 29
Sugamo 巣鴨	I 15	2 · 31
Nishi-sugamo 西巣鴨	I 16	2 · 33
Shin-itabashi 新板橋	I 17	2 · 35
Itabashikuyakushomae 板橋区役所前	I 18	2 · 37
Itabashihoncho 板橋本町	I 19	1 · 38
Motohasunuma 本蓮沼	I 20	2 · 40

Station	Code	No.
Nishi-takashimadaira 西高島平	I 27	2 · 51
Shin-takashimadaira 新高島平	I 26	1 · 49
Takashimadaira 高島平	I 25	2 · 48
Nishidai 西台	I 24	2 · 46
Hasune 蓮根	I 23	2 · 44
Shimura-sanchome 志村三丁目	I 22	2 · 42
Shimura-sakaue 志村坂上	I 21	2 · 42

Shinjuku LINE

The Shinjuku Line connects Shinjuku Station in Shinjuku Ward with Moto-yawata Station in Ichikawa, Chiba Prefecture. It is named for the Shinjuku area of Tokyo, known for its skyscrapers and impressive structures, like the Tokyo Metropolitan Office building, and for the sleepless nightlife district of Kabukicho. It interoperates with the Keio Line.

Keio Line

Station	Lines	Times
S 01	Oedo Line / Marunouchi Line / JR Line / Odakyu Line / Keio Line	
S02	Marunouchi Line / Fukutoshin Line (Open June 2008)	1min1min
S03		2 · 3 ·
S 04	Yurakucho Line / Namboku Line / JR Line	3 · 6 · 4 · 4
S05	Tozai Line / Hanzomon Line	2 · 8 ·
S 06	Mita Line / Hanzomon Line	2 · 10 · 3 · 7
S07	Marunouchi Line (M19) / Chiyoda Line (C12)	2 · 12 ·
S08		1 · 13 ·
S 09	Asakusa Line (A15) / JR Line	2 · 15 · 4 · 11
S10		1 · 16 ·
		2 · 18 · 2 · 13

Shinjuku 新宿

Shinjuku-sanchome 新宿三丁目

Akebonobashi 曙橋

Ichigaya 市ヶ谷

Kudanshita 九段下

Jimbocho 神保町

Ogawamachi 小川町

Iwamotocho 岩本町

Bakuro-yokoyama 馬喰横山

Hamacho 浜町

		Oedo Line

S 11   **Morishita** 森下   1 19·

S12   **Kikukawa** 菊川   2 21·   ● Hanzomon Line

S13   **Sumiyoshi** 住吉   2 23·

S14   **Nishi-ojima** 西大島   2 25·4 17

S 15   **Ojima** 大島   2 27·

S16   **Higashi-ojima** 東大島   2 29·4 21

S 17   **Funabori** 船堀   3 32·

S18   **Ichinoe** 一之江   2 34·

S19   **Mizue** 瑞江   3 37·

S20   **Shinozaki** 篠崎

S 21   **Motoyawata** 本八幡   4 41·9 30   ● JR Line   ○ Keisei Line

Code	Place
S-01	Bunka Fashion College
S-01	Bunka Women's University
S-01	Century Hyatt Tokyo
S-01	JR Shinjuku Building
S-01	JR Tokyo General Hospital
S-01	Keio Plaza Hotel Tokyo
S-01	Kogakuin University
S-01	Shinjuku Post Office
S-01	Shinjuku Prince Hotel
S-01	Takashimaya Times Square
S-01	Tokyo Metropolitan Government
S-02	Hanazono Shinto Shrine
S-02	Shinjuku Gyoen National Garden
S-05	Nippon Budokan
S-06	Kanda Secondhand Book Town
S-07	Ochanomizu Music District
S-07	Ogawamachi Sports Town
S-10	Hamacho Park
S-10	Meijiza Theater
S-11	Fukagawa Edo Museum
S-16	Ojimakomatsugawa Park
S-20	Edogawa River

Oedo LINE

The Oedo Line circles the main area of Tokyo. Tokyo was originally named "Edo," and that's where the Oedo Line gets its name. It runs in a big circle around the city from Tochomae Station to Ryogoku, Daimon, Roppongi and back to Tochomae Station again. A section of it branches off from Tochomae and runs to Hikarigaoka Station in Nerima Ward. The Oedo line is very convenient, you can transfer from it to every subway line in Tokyo except the Chiyoda Line.

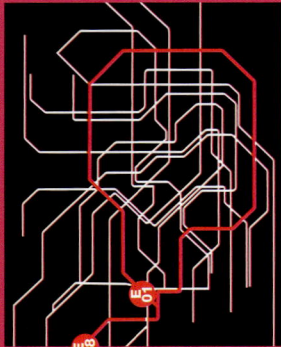

	Marunouchi Line (M08)
	JR Line
	Odakyu Line
	Keio Line
	Seibu Shinjuku Line
	Fukutoshin Line (Open June 2008)
	Tozai Line
	Yurakucho Line
	Namboku Line
	JR Line

Station	Transfers
Shinjuku-nishiguchi 新宿西口	E 01 — 2 / 2
Higashi-shinjuku 東新宿	E 02 — 2 / 4
Wakamatsu-kawada 若松河田	E 03 — 2 / 6
Ushigome-yanagicho 牛込柳町	E 04 — 2 / 8
Ushigome-kagurazaka 牛込神楽坂	E 05 — 2 / 10
Iidabashi 飯田橋	E 06 — 2 / 12

Station	Transfers	
Hikarigaoka 光が丘	E 38	2 / 21
Nerima-kasugacho 練馬春日町	E 37	2 / 19
Toshimaen 豊島園	E 36	2 / 17
Nerima 練馬	E 35	3 / 15 · Seibu Ikebukuro Line
	E 34	2 / 12 · Seibu Yurakucho Line
Shin-egota 新江古田	E 33	3 / 10
Ochiai-minami-nagasaki 落合南長崎		1 / 7

42

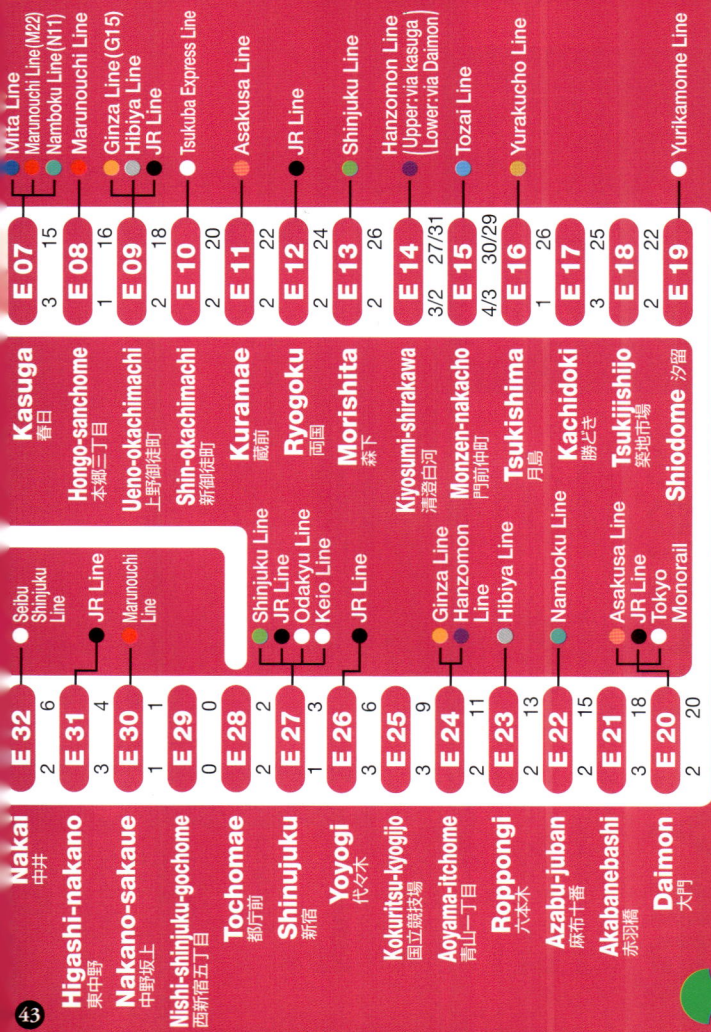

JR Yamanote LINE

The government-owned Japan National Railways (JNR) were privatized on April 1, 1987, and since then they have been run by the Japan Railways (JR) group. The JR Yamanote line is the most important railway line in central Tokyo, as it circles the entire city. It takes about one hour to make its revolution around the city, stopping at major tourist sites like Shinjuku, Harajuku, Tokyo, Ueno, and Ikebukuro.

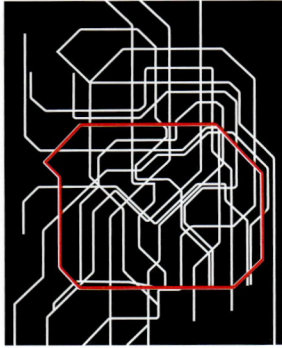

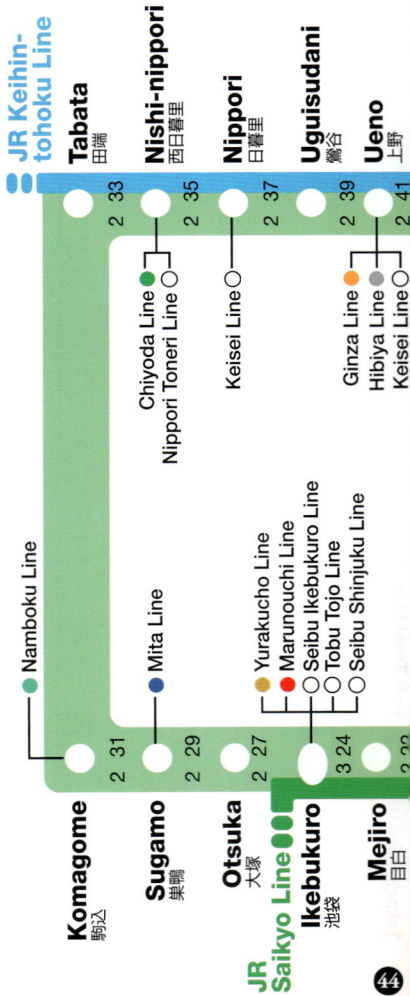

JR Keihin-tohoku Line

Tabata 田端 2 33 ○ Chiyoda Line / Nippori Toneri Line

Nishi-nippori 西日暮里 2 35

Nippori 日暮里 2 37 ○ Keisei Line

Uguisudani 鶯谷 2 39

Ueno 上野 2 41 ○ Ginza Line / Hibiya Line / Keisei Line

Komagome 駒込 2 31

Sugamo 巣鴨 2 29 ● Mita Line

Otsuka 大塚 2 27

● Namboku Line

Ikebukuro 池袋 3 24 ○ Yurakucho Line / Marunouchi Line / ○ Seibu Ikebukuro Line / ○ Tobu Tojo Line / ○ Seibu Shinjuku Line

JR Saikyo Line

Mejiro 目白 2 22

44

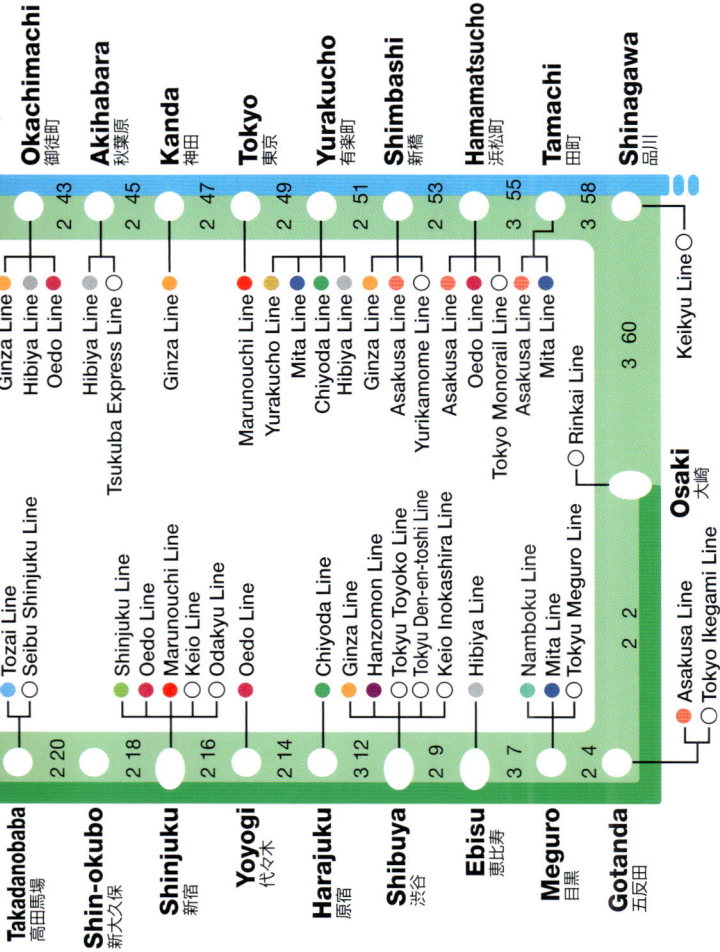

JR Yamanote Line (山手線)

Okachimachi 御徒町 — 2 43
- Ginza Line
- Hibiya Line
- Oedo Line

Akihabara 秋葉原 — 2 45
- Hibiya Line
- Tsukuba Express Line

Kanda 神田 — 2 47
- Ginza Line

Tokyo 東京 — 2 49
- Marunouchi Line

Yurakucho 有楽町 — 2 49
- Yurakucho Line
- Chiyoda Line
- Hibiya Line

Shimbashi 新橋 — 2 51
- Ginza Line
- Asakusa Line
- Yurikamome Line

Hamamatsucho 浜松町 — 2 53
- Asakusa Line
- Oedo Line
- Tokyo Monorail Line

Tamachi 田町 — 3 55
- Asakusa Line
- Mita Line

Shinagawa 品川 — 3 58
- Keikyu Line

Osaki 大崎 — 3 60
- Rinkai Line

3 60

Takadanobaba 高田馬場 — 2 20
- Tozai Line
- Seibu Shinjuku Line

Shin-okubo 新大久保 — 2 18

Shinjuku 新宿 — 2 16
- Shinjuku Line
- Oedo Line
- Marunouchi Line
- Keio Line
- Odakyu Line

Yoyogi 代々木 — 2 14
- Oedo Line

Harajuku 原宿 — 3 12
- Chiyoda Line
- Ginza Line
- Hanzomon Line

Shibuya 渋谷 — 2 9
- Tokyu Toyoko Line
- Tokyu Den-en-toshi Line
- Keio Inokashira Line

Ebisu 恵比寿 — 3 7
- Hibiya Line

Meguro 目黒 — 2 4
- Namboku Line
- Mita Line
- Tokyu Meguro Line

Gotanda 五反田 — 2 2
- Asakusa Line
- Tokyu Ikegami Line

JR Chuo LINE

The JR Chuo Line cuts through the circle of the Yamanote Line and ties together Tokyo Station and Shinjuku Station, continuing on toward Takao. The Chuo Line is an important commuter route for people traveling from western Tokyo to the center of the city. It includes a rapid express that runs especially for commuters. The commuter rapid express stops at Tokyo, Kanda, Ochanomizu, Yotsuya, Shinjuku, Kokubunji, Tachikawa, Hachioji, and Takao. After Takao it stops at every station. The rapid express stops at Tokyo, Kanda, Ochanomizu, Yotsuya, Shinjuku, Nakano, Mitaka, Kokubunji, and Tachikawa. After Tachikawa it stops at every station. The commuter express stops at Tokyo, Kanda, Ochanomizu, Yotsuya, Shinjuku, Nakano, Ogikubo, Kichijoji, Mitaka, Kokubunji, and Tachikawa. After Tachikawa it stops at every station.

Parentheses indicate a weekday only express stop.

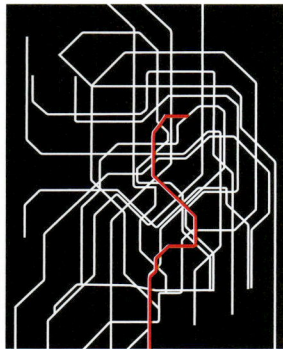

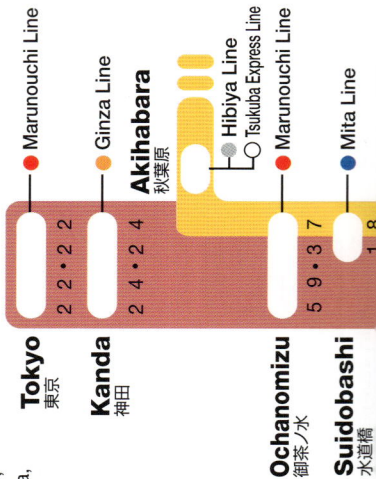

Tokyo 東京
2・2・2 2
● Marunouchi Line

Kanda 神田
2・4・2 4
● Ginza Line

Akihabara 秋葉原
● Hibiya Line
○ Tsukuba Express Line

Ochanomizu 御茶ノ水
5・9・3 7
● Marunouchi Line

Suidobashi 水道橋
1 8
● Mita Line

Top line (left to right)

Station	Connecting Lines	Numbers
	Tozai Line Yurakucho Line Namboku Line Oedo Line	
Iidabashi 飯田橋		3 11
Ichigaya 市ヶ谷	Yurakucho Line Namboku Line Shinjuku Line	2 13
Yotsuya 四ッ谷	Marunouchi Line Namboku Line	5 14・2 15
Shinanomachi 信濃町		1 16
Sendagaya 千駄ヶ谷		2 18
Yoyogi 代々木	Oedo Line	1 20
Shinjuku 新宿	Shinjuku Line Oedo Line	2 20
Okubo 大久保	Marunouchi Line	2 22
	Keio Line Odakyu Line Seibu Shinjuku Line	2 24

JR Sobu Line

Bottom line

To Hachioji, Takao, Otsuki

Station	Connecting Lines	Numbers
Mitaka 三鷹		2 38・2 30
Kichijoji 吉祥寺	Keio Inokashira Line	2 36・2 28
Nishi-ogikubo 西荻窪		3 34・(2) (26)
Ogikubo 荻窪	Marunouchi Line	2 32・2 24
Asagaya 阿佐ヶ谷		2 30・(2) (22)
Koenji 高円寺		2 28・(2) (20)
Nakano 中野	Tozai Line	2 26・4 18
Higashi-nakano 東中野	Oedo Line	

Yokohama-shiei Subway and Minatomirai LINE

From around 1965 Yokohama started to have issues with road congestion, and it became difficult to operate the streetcars and trolley buses that were used for commuting. It was decided that a subway line had to be built to ease the congestion. In 1972, a new line subway line was opened, running 5.2 km from Kamiooka to Isezakichojamachi. Currently, it runs 40.4 km from Azamino to Shonandai, carrying 400,000 people a day through Shin-yokohama, Sakuragicho, Kan-nai, and Totsuka.

The Minatomirai Line runs 4.1 km through 21 districts and runs from Yokohama Station to arrive in Motomachi's Chinatown. It began operating in 2004. It interoperates with the Tokyu Toyoko Line from Yokohama Station and is a highly convenient line that ties together Yokohama with central Tokyo.

Yokohama-shiei Subway

Shonandai 湘南台	**1**	2 2
Shimoiida 下飯田	**2**	3 5
Tateba 立場	**3**	

Minatomirai Line

Katakuracho 片倉町	**23**	2 45
Kishine-koen 岸根公園	**24**	3 48
Mitsuzawa-kamicho 三ツ沢上町	**22**	2 43
Mitsuzawa-shimocho 三ツ沢下町	**21**	2 41
Yokohama 横浜	**20**	● JR Line

Interoperates
Tokyu Toyoko Line

2 50		
Shin-yokohama 新横浜 **25**		
2 52 — JR Line		
26		
2 54 — JR Line		
Kita Shin-yokohama 北新横浜		
Nippa 新羽 **27** — JR Line		
3 56		
Nakamachidai 仲町台 **28**		
3 59		
Center Minami センター南 **29**		
2 62		
Center Kita センター北 **30**		
2 64		
Nakagawa 中川 **31**		
2 66		
Azamino あざみ野 **32**		

2 39
Takashimacho 高島町 **19**
2 37
Sakuragicho 桜木町 **18**
2 35
Kan-nai 関内 **17** — JR Line
1 33
Isezaki-chojamachi 伊勢佐木長者町 **16**
1 32
Bandobashi 阪東橋 **15**
2 31
Yoshinocho 吉野町 **14**
2 29
Maita 蒔田 **13**
3 27
Gumyoji 弘明寺 **12**

1.5 1.5 ◯
Shin-takashima 新高島
1 2.5 ◯
Minatomirai みなとみらい — JR Line
1 3.5 ◯
Bashamichi 馬車道
1 4.5 ◯
Nihon-odori 日本大通り
2 6.5 ◯
Motomachi-Chukagai 元町・中華街

2 7
Nakada 中田 **4**
2 9
Odoriba 踊場 **5**
2 11
Totsuka 戸塚 **6** — JR Line
2 13
Maioka 舞岡 **7**
3 16
Shimonagaya 下永谷 **8**
2 18
Kaminagaya 上永谷 **9**
2 20
Konanchuo 港南中央 **10**
2 22
Kamiooka 上大岡 **11**
2 24

G
M
H
T
C
Y
O
Z
N
A
I
S
E

Exit Finder:

Choose the Right Exit

Akasaka-mitsuke `G 05` `M 13`

- **1** National Diet Building（国会議事堂）
- **2** National Diet Library（国会図書館）
  Shakai Bunka Kaikan（社会文化会館）
- **3** Zenkoku Choson Kaikan（全国町村会館）
  Shakai Bunka Kaikan（社会文化会館）
- **4** Supreme Court of Japan（最高裁判所）
  National Theater（国立劇場）
- **5** Todofuken Kaikan（都道府県会館）
- **6** Sekiyu Kaikan（石油会館）
  Seiryo Kaikan（星陵会館）
- **7** Benkeibashi Bridge（弁慶橋）
  Hotel New Otani（ホテルニューオータニ）
- **8** Akasaka-mitsuke Intersection（赤坂見附交差点）
  Akasaka Excel Hotel Tokyu（赤坂エクセルホテル東急）
  Hie Jinja Shrine（日枝神社）
- **9a** Akasaka Prince Hotel（赤坂プリンスホテル）
- **9b** Todofuken Kaikan（都道府県会館）
- **A** (Akasaka Underground Passageway)（赤坂地下歩道）
  Akasaka-mitsuke Police Box（赤坂見附交番）
- **B** (Akasaka Underground Passageway)（赤坂地下歩道）
  Toyokawa Inari Shrine（豊川稲荷）
- **C** (Akasaka Underground Passageway)（赤坂地下歩道）
  Akasaka Public Parking（赤坂公共駐車場）
- **D** (Akasaka Underground Passageway)（赤坂地下歩道）
  Benkeibashi Bridge（弁慶橋）
  Akasaka Prince Hotel（赤坂プリンスホテル）
  Hotel New Otani（ホテルニューオータニ）
  Nagata-cho Station（永田町駅）
- **Belle Vie Akasaka Exit**（ベルビー赤坂方面出口）
  Belle Vie Akasaka（ベルビー赤坂）
  Akasaka Excel Hotel（赤坂エクセルホテル東急）
  Hie Jinja Shrine（日枝神社）
  Sanno Grand Building（山王グランドビル）
  Prudential Tower（プルデンシャルタワー）

Akihabara `H 15` `JR`

- **1** Mitsui Memorial Hospital（三井記念病院）
- **2** Akihabara Electric City（秋葉原電気街）
- **3** JR Akihabara Station（JR 線秋葉原駅）
  Akihabara Electric City（秋葉原電気街）
- **4** Yasukuni Dori（靖国通り）
- **5** Akihabara Electric City（秋葉原電気街）
  Shinjuku Line Iwamotocho Station（都営新宿線岩本町駅）
  Yasukuni Dori（靖国通り）

Aoyama-itchome `G 04` `Z 03` `E 24`

- **0** Meiji Jingu Shrine Outer Gardens（明治神宮外苑）
  Meiji Kinenkan（明治記念館）
  Kaigakan（絵画館）
- **1** District of Kita-Aoyama（北青山方面）
- **2** District of Moto-Akasaka（元赤坂方面）
  Police Box（交番）
  Akasaka-gosho（赤坂御所）
  Meiji Kinenkan（明治記念館）
  Akasaka Post Office（赤坂郵便局）
  Sogetsu Kaikan（草月会館）
- **3** Aoyama-itchome Intersection（青山一丁目交差点）
  Akasaka Library（区立赤坂図書館）
  Aoyama Cemetery（青山霊園）
  Nogizaka（乃木坂）
- **4** District of Akasaka（赤坂方面）
  Akasaka Post Office（赤坂郵便局）
  Sogetsu Kaikan（草月会館）
  Goethe Institute Tokyo（ドイツ文化会館）
  Hotel Asia Center of Japan（アジア会館）
  Canadian Embassy and Consulate in Japan（カナダ大使館）
  Sanno Hospital（山王病院）
- **5** Aoyama Cemetery（青山霊園）
  The President Hotel Aoyama（ホテルプレジデント青山）

Did you know....?
Roughly 8 million people use the Tokyo subway system every day.

Asakusa G 19   A 18

❶ Sensoji Temple（浅草寺）
Asakusa Kannon（浅草観音）
Kaminarimon（雷門）
Nakamise Dori（仲見世通り）
Rokku Broadway（六区映画演劇街）
Asakusa ROX（浅草ROX）
Asakusa View Hotel（浅草ビューホテル）
Asakusa Hanayashiki Amusement Park（ゆうえんち浅草花やしき）
Demboin Temple（伝法院）
Asakusa Kokaido（浅草公会堂）

❷ Asakusa Bunka Kanko Center（浅草文化観光センター）

❸ Kaminarimon（雷門）
Nakamise Dori（仲見世通り）

❹ Azumabashi Bridge（吾妻橋）
Sumida River（隅田川）
Tokyo Water Cruise Asakusa Terminal（水上バスのりば）
Sumida Park（隅田公園）
Sumida Ward Office（墨田区役所）

❺ Asakusa Station Building（浅草駅ビル）
Edo Dori（江戸通り）
Hakimono Ton-ya Gai（はきもの問屋街）
Tokyo Water Cruise Asakusa Terminal（水上バスのりば）
Kototoibashi（言問橋）

❻ Asakusa Hanayashiki Amusement Park（ゆうえんち浅草花やしき）
Shin-nakamise Dori（新仲見世通り）
Senso-ji Temple（浅草寺）

❼ Matsuya Asakusa（松屋浅草店）
Tobu Asakusa Station（東武浅草駅）

❽ Umamichi Dori（馬道通り）
Edo Dori（江戸通り）
Matsuya Asakusa（松屋浅草店）
Tobu Asakusa Station（東武浅草駅）
Taito Ward Resident Kaikan（台東区民会館）

(A1) Taito Metropolitan Tax Office（台東都税事務所）
Asakusa Post Office（浅草郵便局）
Asakusa Fire Department（浅草消防署）

(A2) Komagatabashi Bridge（駒形橋）

(A3) Kaminarimon Post Office（雷門郵便局）

(A4) Kaminarimon（雷門）
Sensoji Temple（浅草寺）
Nakamise Dori（仲見世通り）
Demboin Temple（伝法院）
Asakusa Kokaido（浅草公会堂）
Taito Ward Office Kaminarimon Branch（台東区役所雷門出張所）
Asakusa Bunka Kanko Center（浅草文化観光センター）

(A5) Tokyo Water Cruise Asakusa Terminal（水上バスのりば）
Azumabashi Bridge（吾妻橋）
Tobu Asakusa Station（東武浅草駅）

Ebisu `H 02` `JR`

(1) JR Ebisu Station（JR 恵比寿駅）
Yebisu Garden Place（恵比寿ガーデンプレイス）
Tokyo Metropolitan Museum of Photography
（東京都写真美術館）
Bus Station（バスのりば）

(2) Shibuyabashi Intersection（渋谷橋交差点）
Meiji Dori（明治通り）

(3) Ebisu Minami-itchome to Ebisu Minami-sanchome
（恵比寿南 1～3 丁目）

(4) Ebisu Park（恵比寿公園）

Ginza `G 09` `M 16` `H 08`

(A1) Ginza-yonchome Intersection（銀座 4 丁目交差点）
San-ai（三愛）
Suzuran Dori（すずらん通り）

Did you know.....?
Highest Station: Kitasenju Station (H21) on the Hibiya Line, at 14.4 m above sea level.

A2 Ginza-yonchome Intersection（銀座４丁目交差点）
San-ai（三愛）
New Melsa（ニューメルサ）
Miyuki Dori（みゆき通り）
Ginza Komatsu（ギンザ・コマツ）

A3 **A4** Sapporo Ginza Building（サッポロ銀座ビル）
Ginza Core（銀座コア）
Matsuzakaya Ginza（銀座松坂屋）
Ginza Gas Hall（銀座ガスホール）
Yamaha Hall（ヤマハホール）
Closed from December 2006, scheduled to reopen Spring 2009

A5 Azuma Dori（あづま通り）

A6 **A7** **A8** **A11** Ginza Mitsukoshi（三越銀座店）

A9 Wako（和光）
Mikimoto（ミキモト）

A10 Wako（和光）

A12 Matsuya Ginza（松屋銀座店）
Oji Hall（王子ホール）
Showa Dori（昭和通り）

A13 Matsuya Ginza（松屋銀座店）

A13 Ito-ya（伊東屋）
Melsa Ginza-2（メルサ Ginza-2）
Tiffany & Co.（ティファニー本店）
Yurakucho Line Ginza-itchome Station（有楽町線銀座一丁目駅）

B1 Wako（和光）

B2 Gucci（グッチ）

B3 [Exit Closed]（閉鎖中）

B4 Ginza Chuo Building（銀座中央ビル）
Namiki Dori（並木通り）

B5 Mikasa Kaikan（三笠会館）
Namiki Dori（並木通り）

B6 Taikakukan Building（対鶴館ビル）

B7 Hermès（メゾン・エルメス）

B8 **B10** Harumi Dori（晴海通り）
Namiki Dori（並木通り）

B8 **B10** Fujiya（不二家）

B9 Sony Building（ソニービル）
Nishi-Ginza Parking（西銀座駐車場）

C1 Ginza Five（銀座ファイブ）
New Tokyo（ニュートーキョー）
Taimei Elementary School（泰明小学校）
Imperial Hotel（帝国ホテル）
Theater District（東宝映画演劇エリア）
Hibiya Chanter（日比谷シャンテ）
Hibiya Park（日比谷公園）

C2 Sukiyabashi Intersection（数寄屋橋交差点）

C3 Mosaic Ginza Hankyu（モザイク銀座阪急）
Toshiba Building（東芝ビル）

C4 Marion（有楽町マリオン）
Yurakucho Hankyu（有楽町阪急）
Yurakucho Seibu（有楽町西武）
JR/Yurakucho Line Yurakucho Station
（JR・有楽町線有楽町駅）

C5 **C7** Nishi-Ginza Department（西銀座デパート）

C6 Tsukamotosozan Building（塚本素山ビル）
Toei Kaikan（東映会館）

C8 Dai-ichi Yayoi Building（第一弥生ビル）
Printemps Ginza（プランタン銀座）
Ginza Church（銀座教会）

C9 Ginza Inz（銀座インズ）
Marunouchi Piccadilly（丸の内ピカデリー）
Printemps Ginza（プランタン銀座）
Marion（有楽町マリオン）
Yurakucho Hankyu（有楽町阪急）
Yurakucho Seibu（有楽町西武）
Kotsu Kaikan（Passport Center）
（交通会館（パスポートセンター））
Tokyo International Forum（東京国際フォーラム）

Did you know.....?
Lowest Station: Roppongi Station (E23) on the Oedo Line, at 42.3 m below sea level.

Hiro-o H 03

1 Gaien-nishi Dori（外苑西通り）
Hiro-o-bashi Intersection（広尾橋交差点）
Arisugawa Memorial Park（有栖川宮記念公園）
Tokyo Metropolitan Library（都立中央図書館）
1 Embassy of the Federal Republic of Germany
（ドイツ連邦共和国大使館）
Embassy of the French Republic（フランス大使館）
2 University of the Sacred Heart（聖心女子大学）
Embassy of the Czech Republic（チェコ共和国大使館）
Embassy of the Slovak Republic（スロヴァキア共和国大使館）
Tokyo Metropolitan Hiro-o Hospital（都立広尾病院）
3 Gaien-Nishi Dori（外苑西通り）
Japanese Red Cross Medical Center（日赤医療センター）
Embassy of Switzerland（スイス大使館）
The Royal Norwegian Embassy（ノルウェー大使館）
Embassy of The People's Republic of China（中国大使館）
Azabu Fire Station（麻布消防署）

Ikebukuro M 25 Y 09 Fukutoshin Line JR

1a 1b Ikebukuro Marui City（マルイシティ池袋店）
Ikebukuro Marui City in the Room（マルイシティインザルーム）
Nishi-Ikebukuro Park（西池袋公園）
Rikkyo University（立教大学）
2a Toshima Tax Office（豊島税務署）
Ikebukuro Police Station（池袋警察署）
2b Tokyo Metropolitan Art Space（東京芸術劇場）
3 4 Hotel Metropolitan（ホテルメトロポリタン）
Nishiguchi Park（西口公園）
Metropolitan Plaza（メトロポリタンプラザ）
5 Tobu Kaikan Annex（東武会館別館）
6 Ikebukuro Tobu Department Store（東武百貨店池袋店）
7 Dai-ichi Nishi-ike Building（第一西池ビル）
8 Tokyo Government Joint Office（都合同庁舎）

9 [Exit Closed]（閉鎖中）

10 - 19 JR West Exit（JR 西口）

13 [Exit Closed]（閉鎖中）

20a 20b 20c JR North Exit（JR 北口）

22 Ikebukuro Parco（池袋パルコ）

23 Intersection in front of JR Higashiguchi Police Station
（東口交番前交差点）

24 25 26 JR East Exit（JR 東口）

27 Higashiguchi Plaza（東口広場）
Ikebukuro Parco（池袋パルコ）

28 [Exit Closed]（閉鎖中）

29 Intersection in front of Higashiguchi Police Station
（東口交番前交差点）

30 Ikebukuro Mitsukoshi（三越池袋店）

33 34 Ikebukuro Mitsukoshi（三越池袋店）
Toshima Ward Office（豊島区役所）
Toshima Public Hall（豊島公会堂）

35 Tokyu Hands（東急ハンズ）
Sunshine City（サンシャインシティ）
Passport Center（パスポートセンター）
Hello Work Ikebukuro（ハローワーク池袋）

36 37 38 Ikebukuro Seibu（池袋西武）

39 Johoku Building（城北ビル）
Minami-Ikebukuro Park（南池袋公園）

40 Kinkado（キンカ堂）

41 42 43 Green-O Dori（グリーン大通り）

C1 Toshima Government Assembly Hall（豊島区民集会室）

C2 Metro City Nishi-Ikebukuro（メトロシティ西池袋）
Tobu Culture School（東武カルチャースクール）

C3 Riviera（リビエラ）
Rikkyo University（立教大学）

C4 C7 Ikebukuro Marui City（マルイシティ池袋店）

C5 C6 Tokiwa Dori（トキワ通り）

C8 West Exit Five-way Intersection（西口五差路）

C9 [Exit Closed]（閉鎖中）

Did you know....?
Old tickets and passes are recycled and used as an ingredient in asphalt for paving roads.

C10 Bunka Dori（文化通り）
Nishi Ichiban Town（西一番街）

Omote-sando `G 02` `C 04` `Z 02`

A1 Hanae Mori Building（ハナエモリビル）
A2 Meiji Jingu Shrine（明治神宮表参道）
Omotesando Hills（表参道ヒルズ）
Anniversaire Omotesando（アニヴェルセル表参道）
Ito Hospital（伊藤病院）
Laforet Harajuku（ラフォーレ原宿）
A3 Omotesando Intersection（表参道交差点）
One Omotesando（ONE 表参道）
Aoyama Bell Commons（青山ベルコモンズ）
A4 Floracion Aoyama（ホテルフロラシオン青山）
A5 Minami-Aoyama 1st Condominiums（南青山第一マンションズ）
Nezu Museum（根津美術館）Closed until 2009（平成21年まで休館中）
From-1st（フロムファースト）
B1 Spiral Building（スパイラルビル）
Aoyama Gakuin University（青山学院大学）
Ogasawara-ryu Kaikan（小原流会館）
Taro Okamoto Memorial Museum（岡本太郎記念館）
B2 United Nations University（国際連合大学）
National Children's Castle（Aoyama Theater）
　　（こどもの城（青山劇場）
Tokyo Women's Plaza（東京ウィメンズプラザ）
B3 Aoyama Rise Square（青山ライズスクエア）
Minami-Aoyama Kaikan（南青山会館）
B4 Omotesando Intersection（表参道交差点）
B5 Meiji Life Insurance Aoyama Parashio
　　（明治生命青山パラシオ）
Aoyama Diamond Hall（青山ダイヤモンドホール）

Roppongi H 04   E 23

- **1a** Azabu Police Station （麻布警察署）
  Piramide （ピラミデ）
- **1b** Roppongi Hills North Tower
      （六本木ヒルズノースタワー）
  Roppongi Zone Building （ZONE 六本木ビル）
- **1c** Roppongi Hills （六本木ヒルズ）
  Virgin Cinemas （ヴァージンシネマズ）
  Grand Hyatt Tokyo （グランドハイアット東京）
  TV Asahi （テレビ朝日）
  Mori Garden （毛利庭園）
  Mori Art Museum （森美術館）
- **2** Roppongi-nanachome （六本木 7 丁目）
  Meiji-ya （明治屋）
  National Art Center, Tokyo （国立新美術館）
- **3** Imoarai Zaka （芋洗坂）
  Roppongi Lapiross （ラピロス六本木）
  Almond （アマンド六本木店）
  Roa Building （ロアビル）
  Ark Hills （アークヒルズ）
  Suntory Hall （テレビ朝日）
  TV Asahi （テレビ朝日）
  ANA Hotel Tokyo （東京全日空ホテル）
  AXIS （アクシス）
- **4a** Roppongi Intersection （六本木交差点）
  Hotel Ibis （ホテルアイビス）
  Tokyo Midtown （東京ミッドタウン）
- **4b** Roppongi Dori （六本木通り）
- **5** Roppongi-sanchome （六本木 3 丁目）
  Iikurakatamachi Intersection （飯倉片町交差点）
  Ark Hills （アークヒルズ）
  Ark Mori Building （アーク森ビル）
  Suntory Hall （サントリーホール）
  TV Asahi （テレビ朝日）
  ANA Hotel Tokyo （東京全日空ホテル）

Did you know.....?
The only subway railway crossing is at the Ueno Railyard near Ueno Station (G16) on the Ginza Line.

6 Police Station（交番）
Haiyuza（俳優座）
7 Chiyoda Line Nogizaka Station（千代田線乃木坂駅）
Tokyo Midtown（東京ミッドタウン）

Shibuya `G 01` `Z 01` `JR`

1 District of The Prime（ザ・プライム方面）
Shibuya 109（シブヤ 109）
2 District of Dogenzaka（道玄坂方面）
Shibuto Cine Tower（渋東シネタワー）
3 Tokyu Hands Shibuya（東急ハンズ渋谷店）
Shibuya Center Town（渋谷センター街）
Shibuya LOFT（渋谷 LOFT）
Shibuya Parco Part 1（渋谷 Parco Part 1）
3a Shibuya 109（シブヤ 109）
Tokyu Department Store（東急本店）
Bunkamura（東急文化村）
4 District of Dogenzaka-shita（道玄坂下方面）
5 Keio Inokashira Line Shibuya Station（京王井の頭線渋谷駅）
Shibuya Mark City（渋谷マークシティ）
Shibuya Excel Hotel Tokyu（渋谷エクセルホテル東急）
6 NHK Studio Park（NHK スタジオパーク）
Shibuya City Office（渋谷区役所）
Seibu Department Store（西武百貨店）
Shibuya PARCO（渋谷パルコ）
Shibuya Marui City（マルイシティ渋谷）
Q FRONT（Q フロント）
7 **7a** District of Jinnan（神南方面）
Shibuya 109-2（シブヤ 109-2）
8 Hachiko-mae Square（ハチ公前広場）
Tokyu Department Store, Toyoko（東急百貨店東横店）
JR/Tokyu Line Shibuya Station（JR・東急線渋谷駅）
9 Shibuya Police Station（渋谷警察署）

9 Tokyu Department Store, Toyoko（東急百貨店東横店）
Tokyu Line Shibuya Station（東急線渋谷駅）
12 Shibuya Police Station（渋谷警察署）
Miyamasuzaka Intersection（宮益坂下交差点）

Shinjuku（Marunouchi Line）M 08 JR

A2 A3 Shinjuku Marui City（マルイシティ新宿）
A4 Kita Building（喜多ビル）
Shinjuku Dori（新宿通り）
A5 Shinjuku Mitsukoshi Alcott（三越本館アルコット）
A6 Nakamuraya（中村屋）
Shinjuku Dori（新宿通り）
A7 Takano（タカノ）
Shinjuku Dori（新宿通り）
A8 LUMINE Est（ルミネエスト）
JR East Exit/Central Exit（JR 東口・中央口）
Hato Bus Station（はとバスのりば）
Takashimaya Times Square（高島屋タイムズスクエア）
A9 LUMINE Est（ルミネエスト）
JR East Exit/Central Exit（JR 東口・中央口）
A10 A11 Metro Underground Food Mall（メトロ食堂街）
A12 A14 JR West Entrance Ticket Gate（JR 西口改札口）
A13 Shinjuku Station Underground Parking（新宿駅地下駐車場）
A15 Underground Plaza（地下広場）
Odakyu Department Store（小田急百貨店）
A18 Shinjuku L-Tower（新宿エルタワー）
Hello Work Shinjuku（ハローワーク新宿）
Tokyo Subcenter District（東京副都心地区）
B1 Shinjuku Line Shinjuku-sanchome Station
（都営新宿線新宿三丁目駅）
B2 Sanwa Toyo Building（新宿三和東洋ビル）
Shinjuku-sanchome Intersection（新宿三丁目交差点）

Did you know.....?
A mammoth was discovered during the construction of Meiji-jingumae Station (C03) on the Chiyoda Line in 1973.

B2 Meiji Dori（明治通り）
Yasukuni Dori（靖国通り）
B3 Isetan（伊勢丹）
Hanazono Shinto shrine（花園神社）
B4 **B5** Isetan（伊勢丹）
B6 Kawase Building （川瀬ビル）
B7 Kinokuniya Building （紀伊國屋ビル）
Shinjuku City Office（新宿区役所）
B8 Sanpokan（三峰館）
B9 Shinjuku Marui Young（マルイヤング新宿）
B10 Subnade（サブナード）
Seibu Shinjuku Station（西武新宿駅）
Shinjuku City Office（新宿区役所）
B11 **B12** Kabukicho（歌舞伎町）
B13 Studio Alta（スタジオアルタ）
Shinjuku Koma Theater（新宿コマ劇場）
B14 Metro Underground Food Mall（メトロ食堂街）
B15 Shinjuku Palette（新宿パレット）
Shinjuku Prince Hotel（新宿プリンスホテル）
B16 **B18** Odakyu Halc（小田急ハルク）
B17 Nishi-shinjuku-itchome（西新宿１丁目）

Shinjuku（Oedo Line, Shinjuku Line）`S 01` `E 27`

A1 JR Tokyo General Hospital （JR 東京総合病院）
Takashimaya Times Square（タカシマヤタイムズスクエア）
2 JR Tokyo General Hospital （JR 東京総合病院）
JR Shinjuku Building （JR 新宿ビル）
5 Shinjuku Post Office（新宿郵便局）
Kogakuin University（工学院大学）
6 Bunka Women's University（文化女子大学）
Bunka Fashion College（文化服飾学院）
7 Keio Plaza Hotel Tokyo（京王プラザホテル）
Kogakuin University（工学院大学）
Tokyo Metropolitan Government（東京都庁）

Tokyo `M 17` `JR`

- **1** Tokyo Metro Otemachi Station （東京メトロ大手町駅）
  Marunouchi Oazo （丸の内オアゾ）
- **2** Yaesu Access Way （八重洲口連絡通路）
- **3** Imperial Palace （皇居）
  Marunouchi Parking （丸の内駐車場）
  Tokyo Metro Nijubashimae Station （東京メトロ二重橋前駅）
- **4** Yaesu Access Way （八重洲口連絡通路）
  Narita Express （成田エクスプレス（NEX））
  JR Line （JR線）
  Tokyo Metro Nijubashimae Station （東京メトロ二重橋前駅）
- **5** Imperial Palace （皇居）
  Tokyo Metro Nijubashimae Station （東京メトロ二重橋前駅）
  Tokyo Central Post Office （東京中央郵便局）
  Marunouchi Building （丸ビル）

Ueno `G 16` `H 17` `JR`

- **1** **2** Ueno Police Station （上野警察署）
  Taito City Office （台東区役所）
  Hello Work Ueno （上野ハローワーク）
  Tokyo Metro Co. （東京地下鉄株式会社）
- **3** **4** Showa Dori （昭和通り）
- **5a** Ueno Marui City （マルイシティ上野）
- **5b** Ameyoko （アメヤ横丁）
- **6** Keisei Ueno Station （京成上野駅）
  Statue of Saigo Takamori （西郷隆盛像）
  Shinobazunoike Pond （しのばずの池）
  Shitamachi Museum （下町風俗資料館）
  Abab （アブアブ）
  Matsuzakaya Ueno （松坂屋上野店）
  Suzumoto Entertainment Hall （鈴本演芸場）
- **7** JR Shinobazu Exit （JR上野駅しのばず口）
  Ueno Park （上野公園）
  Ueno Zoo （上野動物園）

Did you know....?

Certain musicians and performers have been approved by the Tokyo government to play at the following stations on the Oedo Line: Tochomae Station (E28), Shinjuku-nishiguchi Station (E01), and Ueno-okachimachi Station (E09).

7 Ueno Royal Museum（上野の森美術館）
Tokyo Bunka Kaikan（東京文化会館）
National Museum of Western Art（国立西洋美術館）
National Science Museum, Tokyo（国立科学博物館）
Tokyo National Museum（東京国立博物館）
Tokyo Metropolitan Art Museum（東京都美術館）

8 Atre Ueno（アトレ上野）
Central Plaza of JR Ueno Station（JR上野駅中央広場）

9 Atre Ueno（アトレ上野）
JR Central Exit/Asakusa Exit（JR上野駅正面口・浅草口）

Landmark Finder:

Find
the Nearest
Station

Public Offices
Theaters, Stadiums, Auditoriums
Museums
Places of Worship
Parks, Gardens, Zoos
Shopping Streets
Hotels

Public Offices

National Diet Building（国会議事堂）`M14` `C07`

Tokyo Metropolitan Government Buildings（東京都庁）`E28`

Japan Patent Office（特許庁）
`G06` `G07` `M14` `M15` `H06` `C07` `C08` `N06`

Supreme Court of Japan（最高裁判所）
`Y16` `Z04` `N07`

State Guesthouse（迎賓館）`M12` `N08`

Japan Meteorological Agency（気象庁）
`M18` `T08` `C11` `Z08` `I09`

Theaters, Stadiums, Auditoriums

Asakusa Entertainment Hall（浅草演芸ホール）
`G19` `A18`

Asakusa Kokaido（浅草公会堂）`G19` `A18`

Bunkamura（東急文化村）`G01` `Z01`

Imperial Theater（帝国劇場）`H07` `C09` `Y18` `I08`

Kabuki-za Theater（歌舞伎座）`H09` `A11`

Kokugikan（両国国技館）`E12`

Koma Stadium（新宿コマ劇場）`M08` `E01`

Kudan Kaikan（九段会館）`T07` `Z06` `S05`

Meijiza Theater（明治座）`H13` `Z10` `A14` `S10`

Nakano Sunplaza（中野サンプラザ）`T01`

National Children's Castle（Aoyama Theater）
（こどもの城（青山劇場））`G02` `C04` `Z02`

National Theater（国立劇場）`Y16` `Z04` `Z05` `N07`

Nippon Budokan（日本武道館）`T07` `Z06` `S05`

Sogetsu Kaikan（草月会館）`G04` `Z03` `E24`

Suntory Hall（サントリーホール）`N05`

Suzumoto Entertainment Hall（鈴本演芸場）
`G15` `H16` `E09`

Tokyo Big Sight（東京ビッグサイト）
`G08` `A10`（transfer to Yurikamome Line at
Shimbashi Station）
`Y22`（transfer to Yurikamome Line at Toyosu
Station）
`Y24`（transfer to Rinkai Line at Shin-kiba
Station）

Tokyo Dome CIty（東京ドームシティ）`M22` `N11`

Tokyo International Forum（東京国際フォーラム）
`Y18`

Tokyo Metropolitan Art Space（東京芸術劇場）
`M25` `Y09`

Tokyo Takarazuka Theater（東京宝塚劇場）
`H07` `C09` `Y18` `I18`

Museums

Bridgestone Museum of Art（ブリヂストン美術館）`G 10`

Edo-Tokyo Museum（江戸東京博物館）`E 12`

Fukagawa Edo Museum（深川江戸資料館）
`S 11` `E 13` `E 14` `Z 11`

Laforet Museum Harajuku（ラフォーレミュージアム）
`H 05` `N 05`

Mori Art Museum（森美術館）`H 04` `E 23`

Museum of Contemporary Art Tokyo
（東京都現代美術館）`E 14` `Z 11`

National Science Museum, Tokyo
（国立科学博物館）`G 16` `H 17`

Ota Memorial Museum（太田記念美術館）`C 03`

Science Museum（科学技術館）
`S 05` `Z 06` `T 07` `T 08`

Subway Museum（地下鉄博物館）`T 17`

Taro Okamoto Memorial Museum（岡本太郎記念館）
`G 02` `C 04` `Z 02`

Tokyo Metropolitan Art Museum（東京都美術館）
`G 16` `H 17`

Tokyo Metropolitan Teien Art Museum
（東京都庭園美術館）`N 02` `I 02`

Tokyo National Museum（東京国立博物館）
`G 16` `H 17`

Ueno Royal Museum （上野の森美術館） `G16` `H17`

Places of Worship

Demboin Temple （伝法院） `G19` `A18`

Hanazono Shinto Shrine （花園神社） `M09` `S02`

Hie Jinja Shrine （日枝神社） `G06` `N06`

Higashi-honganji Temple （東京本願寺） `G18`

Kaminarimon （雷門） `G19` `A18`

Kan-eiji Temple （寛永寺） `G16` `H17`

Meiji Jingu Shrine （明治神宮） `C03`

Nicholai-do （ニコライ堂） `C12`

Sensoji Temple （浅草寺） `G19` `A18`

Suitengu Shrine （水天宮） `Z10` `H13` `A14`

Tomioka Hachimangu Shrine （富岡八幡宮）
`T12` `E15`

Toshogu Shrine （東照宮） `G16` `H17`

Tsukiji Honganji Temple （築地本願寺） `H10`

Yushima Temple （湯島聖堂） `M20`

Yushima Temmangu Shrine （湯島天満宮） `C13`

Zojoji Temple （増上寺） `I05` `A09` `E20`

Parks, Gardens, Zoos

Arisugawa Memorial Park（有栖川宮記念公園）
`N04` `E22`

Asakusa Hanayashiki Amusement Park
（ゆうえんち浅草花やしき）`G19` `A18`

Happo-en Garden（八芳園）`N02` `I02`

Hamarikyu Onshi Teien（浜離宮恩賜庭園）
`G08` `A10` `E19`

Hibiya Park（日比谷公園）`H07` `C08` `M15` `I07`

Imperial Palace/Nijubashi（皇居外苑（二重橋））
`C10` `I08` `Y18` `H07`

Kiba Park（木場公園）`T13`

Kiyosumi Teien Garden（清澄庭園）`Z11` `E14`

Koishikawa-Korakuen（小石川後楽園）`M22` `N11`

Kyu-Furukawa Teien Garden（旧古河庭園）`N15`

Kyu-Iwasaki-tei Teien（旧岩崎邸庭園）`C13`

Kyu-Shibarikyu Onshi Teien Garden
（旧芝離宮恩賜庭園）`A09` `E20`

Megurogajo-en Garden（目黒雅叙園）`N01` `I01`

Meiji Jingu Shrine Outer Gardens（明治神宮外苑）
`G03` `G04` `Z03` `E25` `E24`

Ojimakomatsugawa Park（大島小松川公園）`S16`

Rikugi-en Garden（六義園）`N14`

Shinjuku Gyoen National Garden（新宿御苑）
`M10` `S02` `E25`

Sotobori Park（外濠公園）`M12` `N08`

Sumida Park（隅田公園）`G19` `A18`

Sunshine International Aquarium
（サンシャイン国際水族館）`Y10`

Tokyo Sea Life Park（葛西臨海水族園）`T17`

Tokyo Tower/Shiba Park（東京タワー／芝公園）
`H05` `I05` `E21`

Ueno Onshi Park（Shinobazunoike Pond）
（上野恩賜公園（不忍池））`G16` `H17` `C13`

Ueno Zoo（上野動物園）`G16` `H17`

Yoyogi Park（代々木公園）`C02` `C03`

Zoshigaya Reien（雑司ヶ谷霊園）`Y10`

🛍️ Shopping Streets

Akihabara Electric City（秋葉原電気街）`G14` `H15`

Ameyoko（アメ横）`G15` `G16` `E09`

Azabu Juban Shopping Town（麻布十番商店街）
`N04` `E22`

Coredo Nihombashi（コレド日本橋）`G11` `T10` `A13`

Daikanyama（代官山）`H01`

Kabukicho（歌舞伎町）`M08` `S01` `E01`

Kappabashi Dogugai Street（かっぱ橋道具街）
`G18` `H18`

Laforet Harajuku（ラフォーレ原宿）`C03`

Meiji Jingu Shrine Omotesando（明治神宮表参道）
`G02` `C03` `C04` `Z02`

Nakamise Dori（仲見世通り）`G19` `A18`

Omotesando Hills（表参道ヒルズ）`G02` `C04` `Z02`

Roppongi Hills（六本木ヒルズ）`H04` `E23`

Shibuya Center Town（渋谷センター街）`G01` `Z01`

SHIBUYA109（渋谷 109）`G01` `Z01`

Sugamo-Jizo-Dori Shopping Center（巣鴨商店街）
`I15`

Sunshine City（サンシャインシティ）`Y10`

Takashimaya Times Square
（タカシマヤタイムズスクエア）`M08` `S01`

Takeshita Dori（竹下通り）`C03`

Tsukiji Market（築地市場）`E18` `H10`

 **Hotels**

Akasaka Prince Hotel（赤坂プリンスホテル）
`G05` `M13` `Y16` `Z04` `N07`

ANA Hotel Tokyo（東京全日空ホテル）`G06` `N06`

Century Hyatt Tokyo（センチュリーハイアット東京）
`M 07` `E 28`

Four Seasons Hotel Tokyo at Chinzan-so
（フォーシーズンズホテル椿山荘東京） `Y 12`

Four Seasons Hotel Tokyo at Marunouchi
（フォーシーズンズホテル丸の内東京） `M 17`

Hilton Tokyo（ヒルトン東京） `M 07` `E 28`

Hotel New Otani（ホテルニューオータニ）
`G 05` `M 13` `Y 15` `Z 04` `N 07`

Imperial Hotel（帝国ホテル） `M 16` `H 07` `C 09` `I 07`

Keio Plaza Hotel Tokyo（京王プラザホテル）
`M 08` `S 01` `E 28`

Mandarin Oriental（マンダリンホテルオリエンタル）
`G 12` `Z 09`

Palace Hotel Tokyo（パレスホテル）
`M 18` `T 09` `C 11` `Z 08` `I 09`

Park Hyatt Tokyo（パークハイアット東京） `E 28`

Radisson Miyako Hotel Tokyo
（ラディソン都ホテル） `N 02` `N 03` `I 02` `I 03`

Shinjuku Prince Hotel（新宿プリンスホテル）
`M 08` `E 01`

Sofitel Tokyo（ソフィテル東京） `C 13`

Takanawa Prince Hotel（高輪プリンスホテル） `A 06`

Tokyo Prince Hotel（東京プリンスホテル）
`A 09` `I 06` `E 20`

Westin Tokyo（ウエスティンホテル東京） `H 02`

Useful Japanese Words and Phrases

Everyday Phrases

Yes.
はい。
Hai.

No.
いいえ。
Iie.

Hello.
こんにちは。
Kon-nichi wa.

Nice to meet you.
はじめまして。
Hajime-mashite.

Thank you.
ありがとう。
Arigato.

You are welcome.
どういたしまして。
Do itashi-mashite.

Goodbye.
さようなら。
Sayonara.

Excuse me. (addressing)
すみません。
Sumimasen.

Excuse me.
しつれいします。
Shitsurei shimasu.

I'm sorry.
ごめんなさい。
Gomen-nasai.

Useful Phrases

How much is the fare to Shinjuku?
しんじゅくまではいくらですか。
Shinjuku made wa ikura desu ka.

Could I have a subway map?
ちかてつのろせんずをもらえますか。
Chikatetsu no rosenzu wo morae-masu ka.

Where is the elevator?
エレベーターはどこですか。
Elebeta wa doko desu ka.

Where is the restroom?
トイレはどこですか。
Toire wa doko desu ka.

Where should I change trains?
のりかえはどこですか。
Norikae wa doko desu ka.

How long does it take to get to Shibuya Station?
しぶやまでどれくらいでつきますか。
Shibuya made dore kurai de tsuki-masu ka.

Which train should I take to go to Akihabara Station?
あきはばらへはどのでんしゃにのればいいですか。
Akihabara e wa dono densha ni nore-ba ii desu ka.

Does this train stop at Roppongi?
このでんしゃはろっぽんぎにとまりますか。
Kono densha wa Roppongi ni tomari-masu ka.

How many stops to Ginza station?
ぎんざえきはいくつめですか。
Ginza eki wa ikutsume desu ka.

I lost my ticket.
きっぷをなくしました。
Kippu o nakushi-mashita.

Could you please say that again?
もういちどいってください。
Moichido itte kudasai.

Travel Terms

subway
地下鉄／ちかてつ
chikatetsu

station
駅／えき
eki

Ginza Line
銀座線／ぎんざせん
ginza sen

gate
改札／かいさつ
kaisatsu

automatic ticket gate
自動改札／じどうかいさつ
jido kaisatsu

bound for ～
～方面／ほうめん
homen

automatic ticket vending machine
自動券売機／じどうけんばいき
jido kenbaiki

ticket
切符／きっぷ
kippu

fare
運賃／うんちん
unchin

change
おつり
otsuri

station attendant
駅係員／えきかかりいん
eki kakariin

entrance
入口／いりぐち
iriguchi

exit
出口／でぐち
deguchi

fare adjustment
精算／せいさん
seisan

information desk
案内所／あんないじょ
annaijo

station office
駅事務室／えきじむしつ
eki-jimushitsu

lost & found
忘れ物／わすれもの
wasuremono

pass office
定期券売り場／ていきけんうりば
teikiken uriba

subway map
路線図／ろせんず
rosenzu

right
右／みぎ
migi

left
左／ひだり
hidari

north
北／きた
kita

south
南／みなみ
minami

west
西／にし
nishi

east
東／ひがし
higashi

Useful Numbers and Links

Emergency

Police	110
Police (for English calls)	03-3501-0110
Ambulance	119
Fire	119

Tourist Information

Tokyo Tourist Information Center

@ Tokyo Metropolitan Government Building	03-5321-3077
@ Haneda Airport	03-5757-9345
@ Keisei Ueno	03-3836-3471

Tokyo Tourism Info
http://www.tourism.metro.tokyo.jp/english/

Transportation

Tokyo Metro   03-3941-2004
http://www.tokyometro.jp/e/index.html

Toei Transportation   03-3816-5700
http://www.kotsu.metro.tokyo.jp/english/index.html

Tokyo International Airport (Haneda Airport) 03-5757-8111
http://www.tokyo-airport-bldg.co.jp/fl/english/index.html

Narita International Airport   0476-34-5000
http://www.narita-airport.jp/en/index.html

Kansai International Airport   0724-55-2500
http://www.kansai-airport.or.jp/en/index.asp

JR East   050-2016-1603
http://www.jreast.co.jp/e/index.html

Lost & Found

Tokyo Metro	03-3834-5577
Toei Transportation	03-3812-2011
JR East	050-2016-1603
Taxi	03-3648-0300

Signs and Symbols

Mobile Manner Mode
携帯マナーモード

Courtesy Seats
優先席

Information
情報コーナー

Question and Answer
案内所

Restroom
お手洗い

Men's Restroom
男性お手洗い

Women's Restroom
女性お手洗い

Accessible Facility
身体障害者使用可能設備

Nursery
乳幼児用設備

Ostomate
オストメイト

Elevator
エレベーター

Escalator
エスカレーター

Stairs
階段

Tokyo Metro Tickets ／
Fare Adjustment
きっぷうりば／精算所

Tokyo Metro Pass Office
定期券うりば

Lost & Found
忘れ物

Tokyo Metro Station Office
駅事務所／お忘れ物取扱所

Telephone
電話

Coin Lockers
ロッカー

Other Train Lines
他社線

No Smoking
禁煙

No Mobiles
携帯電話使用禁止

No Admittance
立入禁止

SOS
Emergency Telephone
非常電話

SOS
Emergency Call Button
非常ボタン

Airport Access Information

Narita International Airport (Narita Airport)	**JR**	JR Rapid service	90 min	¥1,280	**Tokyo Station**
		JR Narita Express	60 min	¥2,940	
		JR Narita Express	80 min	¥3,110	**Shinjuku Station**
		JR Narita Express	90 min	¥3,110	**Ikebukuro Station**
		JR Narita Express	90 min	¥4,180	**Yokohama Station**
	Keisei Line	Keisei Skyliner	51 min	¥1,920	**Nippori Station**
		Keisei Skyliner	56 min	¥1,920	**Ueno Station**
		Keisei Limited Express	67 min	¥1,000	**Nippori Station**
		Keisei Limited Express	71 min	¥1,000	**Ueno Station**
		Airport Limousine Bus	60–90 min	¥3,000–¥3,100	**Major Tokyo Hotels**
		Airport Limousine Bus	55 min	¥3,000	**Tokyo City Air Terminal**
		Airport Limousine Bus	75 min	¥3,100	**Tokyo International Airport (Haneda)**

Tokyo International Airport (Haneda Airport)	Airport Limousine Bus		40–60 min	¥1,000–¥1,200		**Major Tokyo Hotels**
	Airport Limousine Bus		25–35 min	¥900		**Tokyo City Air Terminal**
	Airport Limousine Bus		40 min	¥900		**Tokyo Station**
	Keihin Express	19 min ¥400	**Shinagawa Station**	JR 9 min ¥160		**Tokyo Station**
	Tokyo Monorail	22 min ¥470	**Hamamatsucho Station**	JR 4 min ¥150		

FAQ

Q: When is rush hour?

A: The trains are extremely crowded from about 8:00 AM to 9:00 AM.

Q: What does the "Women Only" sign mean?

A: It indicates that a car that is reserved for women only. Only women are allowed to board these cars on the Hibiya Line, Tozai Line, Chiyoda Line, Yurakucho Line, Hanzomon Line, and Shinjuku Line during weekday morning rush hour. If you are on any of these lines during the rush hour, make sure you know what car you're getting on.

Q: Am I allowed to use my phone on the train?

A: The following rules apply:

Put your phone on manner mode and don't talk on the phone on the train.

Turn your phone off when you are near the courtesy seats. Courtesy seats are special seats reserved for the elderly, handicapped persons, pregnant women, and injured persons.

Q: What if there is an accident while I am on the subway?

A: Do not try to exit the train car. Wait for the train announcement, and then calmly follow the directions. If you do not understand Japanese, watch what the other passengers are doing and follow them.

Q: What if I forget something on the train?

A: As soon as you realize you've lost something, contact the nearest station. The station will keep your lost item for one day.

If it is more than one day since you lost the item, try the following numbers:

Tokyo Metro Lost & Found Center   03-3834-5577
Monday through Friday, 9:30 – 19:00
Saturday and holidays, 9:30 – 16:00
Closed on Sundays
Toei Subways   03-3812-2011
Monday through Friday, 9:00 – 19:00
Saturday, Sunday and holidays, 9:00 – 17:00

When you go to pick up your lost item, bring identification and a personal seal (if you have one).

Q: What if I buy the wrong ticket?

A: You can get a refund for regular tickets, street car and bus tickets, Toei Subway one-day tickets, and Tokyo Metro one-day open tickets—however, it is not a full refund. There is a service charge of ¥160 for Tokyo Metro regular tickets, ¥170 for Toei Subway regular tickets, ¥210 for one-day open tickets on both lines, and ¥210 for transfer tickets.

Coupon Tickets

Lost coupon tickets that are still valid can be refunded for the purchase value minus the prorated value of the number of tickets used and a ¥210 service charge.

Rail Passes

Lost rail passes that are still valid can be refunded for the pass value minus the prorated value of the number of months used and a ¥210 service charge.

Q: What if I travel further than the fare I paid for?

A: You must pay for the difference between your proper fare and that of the actual ticket you bought. If you mistakenly paid more than the required fare, you cannot get a refund.

Q: Can I take my bicycle onto the train? What are other restrictions on items?

A: If the bicycle is collapsible or can be taken apart and put in a bag, and is within the permitted weight and dimensions for carry-ons, it can accompany you free of charge. You are allowed to carry up to two items each with a total height, width, and length under 250 cm and weight under 30 kg (However, items exceeding 200 cm long in any one dimension are prohibited.) Pets are allowed on the train if they are in carriers and are not a nuisance to other passengers. Wild animals and snakes are not allowed on the train under any circumstances. You can carry umbrellas, canes, shoulder bags, and sports equipment if completely put in a case.

The following items are prohibited, regardless of size: Hazardous materials, heaters/burners, corpses, explosives, poisons, volatile chemicals, animals (other than those that are carry-ons), dirty or offensive-smelling items that could damage the train.

Q: What do the letters and numbers mean on the route maps displayed on the station platforms?

A: This is the Station Numbering System. For each station marker, the letter at the top signifies the name of the train line, and the number below identifies the station on that line. At the front of this book is a train map showing the station numbers.

INFORMATION DESKS

Tokyo Metro Customer Relations
Tel 03-3941-2004
Hours: 9:00–20:00

Toei Subway Information
Tel 03-3816-5700
Hours: 9:00–19:00

Index of Stations

C02	Yoyogi-koen	代々木公園	よよぎこうえん	28
C03	Meiji-jingumae	明治神宮前	めいじじんぐうまえ	28
C04	Omote-sando	表参道	おもてさんどう	28
C05	Nogizaka	乃木坂	のぎざか	28
C06	Akasaka	赤坂	あかさか	28
C07	Kokkai-gijidomae	国会議事堂前	こっかいぎじどうまえ	28
C08	Kasumigaseki	霞ケ関	かすみがせき	28
C09	Hibiya	日比谷	ひびや	28
C10	Nijubashimae	二重橋前	にじゅうばしまえ	28
C11	Otemachi	大手町	おおてまち	29
C12	Shin-ochanomizu	新御茶ノ水	しんおちゃのみず	29
C13	Yushima	湯島	ゆしま	29
C14	Nezu	根津	ねづ	29
C15	Sendagi	千駄木	せんだぎ	29
C16	Nishi-nippori	西日暮里	にしにっぽり	29
C17	Machiya	町屋	まちや	29
C18	Kita-senju	北千住	きたせんじゅ	29
C19	Ayase	綾瀬	あやせ	29
C20	Kita-ayase	北綾瀬	きたあやせ	29

Yurakucho Line 有楽町線 `30, 31`

Y01	Wakoshi	和光市	わこうし	30
Y02	Chikatetsu-narimasu	地下鉄成増	ちかてつなります	30
Y03	Chikatetsu-akatsuka	地下鉄赤塚	ちかてつあかつか	30
Y04	Heiwadai	平和台	へいわだい	30
Y05	Hikawadai	氷川台	ひかわだい	30
Y06	Kotake-mukaihara	小竹向原	こたけむかいはら	30
Y07	Senkawa	千川	せんかわ	30
Y08	Kanamecho	要町	かなめちょう	30
Y09	Ikebukuro	池袋	いけぶくろ	30
Y10	Higashi-ikebukuro	東池袋	ひがしいけぶくろ	30
Y11	Gokokuji	護国寺	ごこくじ	31
Y12	Edogawabashi	江戸川橋	えどがわばし	31
Y13	Iidabashi	飯田橋	いいだばし	31
Y14	Ichigaya	市ケ谷	いちがや	31
Y15	Kojimachi	麹町	こうじまち	31
Y16	Nagatacho	永田町	ながたちょう	31
Y17	Sakuradamon	桜田門	さくらだもん	31
Y18	Yurakucho	有楽町	ゆうらくちょう	31
Y19	Ginza-itchome	銀座一丁目	ぎんざいっちょうめ	31
Y20	Shintomicho	新富町	しんとみちょう	31
Y21	Tsukishima	月島	つきしま	31
Y22	Toyosu	豊洲	とよす	31
Y23	Tatsumi	辰巳	たつみ	31
Y24	Shin-kiba	新木場	しんきば	31

Fukutoshin Line 副都心線 `30`

	Wakoshi	和光市	わこうし	30
	Chikatetsu-narimasu	地下鉄成増	ちかてつなります	30
	Chikatetsu-akatsuka	地下鉄赤塚	ちかてつあかつか	30
	Heiwadai	平和台	へいわだい	30
	Hikawadai	氷川台	ひかわだい	30

	Kotake-mukaihara	小竹向原	こたけむかいはら	30
	Senkawa	千川	せんかわ	30
	Kanamecho	要町	かなめちょう	30
	Ikebukuro	池袋	いけぶくろ	30
	Zoshigaya	雑司が谷	ぞうしがや	30
	Nishi-waseda	西早稲田	にしわせだ	30
	Higashi-shinjuku	東新宿	ひがし␣しんじゅく	30
	Shinjuku-sanchome	新宿三丁目	しんじゅくさんちょうめ	30
	Kita-sando	北参道	きたさんどう	30
	Meiji-jingumae	明治神宮前	めいじじんぐうまえ	30
	Shibuya	渋谷	しぶや	30

Hanzomon Line 半蔵門線 `32, 33`

Z01	Shibuya	渋谷	しぶや	32
Z02	Omote-sando	表参道	おもてさんどう	32
Z03	Aoyama-itchome	青山一丁目	あおやまいっちょうめ	32
Z04	Nagatacho	永田町	ながたちょう	32
Z05	Hanzomon	半蔵門	はんぞうもん	32
Z06	Kudanshita	九段下	くだんした	32
Z07	Jimbocho	神保町	じんぼうちょう	32
Z08	Otemachi	大手町	おおてまち	33
Z09	Mitsukoshimae	三越前	みつこしまえ	33
Z10	Suitengumae	水天宮前	すいてんぐうまえ	33
Z11	Kiyosumi-shirakawa	清澄白河	きよすみしらかわ	33
Z12	Sumiyoshi	住吉	すみよし	33
Z13	Kinshicho	錦糸町	きんしちょう	33
Z14	Oshiage	押上	おしあげ	33

Nambuku Line 南北線 `34, 35`

N01	Meguro	目黒	めぐろ	34
N02	Shirokanedai	白金台	しろかねだい	34
N03	Shirokane-takanawa	白金高輪	しろかねたかなわ	34
N04	Azabu-juban	麻布十番	あざぶじゅうばん	34
N05	Roppongi-itchome	六本木一丁目	ろっぽんぎいっちょうめ	34
N06	Tameike-sanno	溜池山王	ためいけさんのう	34
N07	Nagatacho	永田町	ながたちょう	34
N08	Yotsuya	四ツ谷	よつや	34
N09	Ichigaya	市ケ谷	いちがや	34
N10	Iidabashi	飯田橋	いいだばし	34
N11	Korakuen	後楽園	こうらくえん	35
N12	Todaimae	東大前	とうだいまえ	35
N13	Hon-komagome	本駒込	ほんこまごめ	35
N14	Komagome	駒込	こまごめ	35
N15	Nishigahara	西ケ原	にしがはら	35
N16	Oji	王子	おうじ	35
N17	Oji-kamiya	王子神谷	おうじかみや	35
N18	Shimo	志茂	しも	35
N19	Akabane-iwabuchi	赤羽岩淵	あかばねいわぶち	35

Asakusa Line 浅草線 `36, 37`

A01	Nishi-magome	西馬込	にしまごめ	36
A02	Magome	馬込	まごめ	36

Index **91**

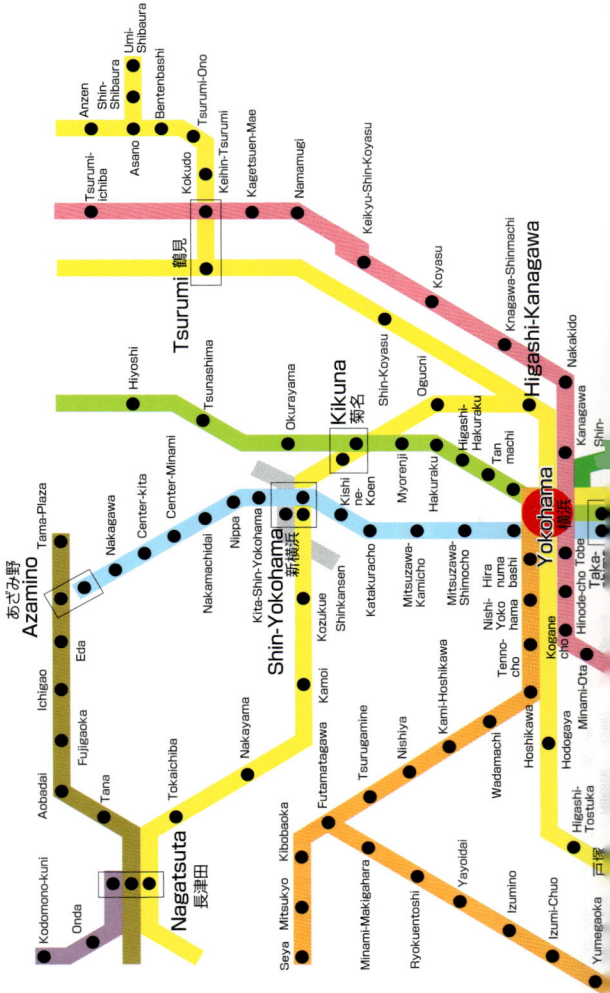

Yokohama City Area Railway and Subway Map

Legend:

- JR Line (Tokaido, Yokosuka, Keihin-tohoku, Yokohama)
  JR線 (東海道線、横須賀線、京浜東北線、横浜線)
- Keihinkyuko Line
  京浜急行線
- Soutetsu Line
  相鉄線
- Yokohama-shiei Subway
  横浜市営地下鉄
- Tokyu Toyoko Line
  東急東横線
- Tokyu Den-en-toshi Line
  東急田園都市線
- Kodomonokuni Line
  こどもの国線
- Seasaide Line
  シーサイドライン
- Minatomirai Line
  みなとみらい線

Stations:

Minatomirai, Bashamichi, Nihon-oodori, Motomachi-China town

Takashimacho 高島町, Sakuragicho 桜木町, Kannai 関内, Ishikawacho

Isezaki-Choja machi, Bando bashi, Yamate

Yoshino cho, Maita

Kami-Ooka 上大岡, Gumyoji, Gumyoji

Shin-Sugita 新杉田, Negishi, Isogo

Namiki-Kita, Namiki-Chuo, Sachiura, Sanyoshinko-Center

Byoubu gaura, Sugita, Tori hama, Nambu-Shijo, Shidai-igakubu, Fukuura

Kami-Nagaya, Konandai, Yokoudai, Keikyu-Tomioka, Kanazawa-Bunko, Hakkeijima

Maioka, Hongodai, Noukendai, Nojima-Koen, Uminokoen-Shibaguchi

Tateba, Odoriba, Ofuna, Kanazawa-Hakkei 金沢八景, Uminokoen-Minamiguchi, Mutsuura

Nagaya

idogaya

横浜観光コンベンション・ビューロー
www.welcome.city.yokohama.jp

The Little Tokyo Subway Guidebook:
Everything You Need to Know to Get Around the City and Beyond

2007年3月6日　第1刷発行

編　者　　IBCパブリッシング

監　修　　東京地下鉄株式会社
　　　　　東京都交通局

発行者　　賀川　洋

発行所　　IBCパブリッシング株式会社
　　　　　〒107-0051 東京都港区元赤坂1-1-8,赤坂コミュニティビル5F
　　　　　www.ibcpub.co.jp

発売元　　日本洋書販売株式会社　Tel. 03-5786-7420

デザイン　川原田　良一

資料協力　東日本旅客鉄道株式会社
　　　　　財団法人横浜観光コンベンション・ビューロー

印刷所　　株式会社シナノ

ISBN978-4-89684-457-3

Railway Route Map — East Japan Railway Company

Major line labels:
- ❶ Joetsu Line
- ❶ Takasaki Line
- ❸ Shonan-Shinjuku Line
- ⑯ Saikyo Line, Kawagoe Line-Rinkai Line through service
- ⑪ Chuo Line [Rapid Service]
- ⑳ Musashino Line · Keiyo Line
- ⑯ Hachiko Line
- Kawagoe Line · Hachiko Line
- ⑭ Ome Line
- ⑪ Itsukaichi Line
- ⑩ Chuo Line
- ❺ Sagami Line
- ❼ Nambu Line
- ❻ Yokohama Line · Negishi Line
- ❶ Tokaido Line
- ❸ Shonan-Shinjuku Line
- ❸ Ito Line
- ❷ Yokosuka Line · Sobu Line

Station/area labels (selection):
Shibukawa, Agatsuma Line, Yagihara, Maebashi, Maebashi-oshima, Komagata, Isesaki, Iwajuku, Kiryu, Omata, Yamaenma, Ashikaga, Tomita, Sano, Iwafu
Shim-Maebashi, Takasaki, Kumagaya, Omiya, Kita-Urawa, Musashi-Urawa
Honjowaseda, Kawagoe, Hachioji, Tachikawa, Nishi-Kokubunji, Kokubunji
Hatsukari, Sasago, Otsuki, Saruhashi, Torisawa, Yamanashi, Shiotsu, Uenohara, Fujino, Sagamiko, Yose, Takao, Nishi-Hachioji, Hachioji-minamino, Katakura
Kai-Yamato, Katsunumabudokyo, Enzan, Higashi-Yamanashi, Yamanashishi, Kasugaicho, Isawa-Onsen, Sakaori
Kofu, Minobu Line, Ryuo, Shiozaki, Nirasaki
Hashimoto, Fuchuhommachi, Yoyogi, Shibuya
Atami, Yugawara, Manazuru, Odawara, Kozu, Chigasaki, Ofuna, Yokohama, Higashi-Kanagawa
Shin-Yokohama, Shin-Kawasaki, Tsurumi

Legend

- ❶ Tokaido Line
- ❷ Yokosuka Line · Sobu Line [Rapid Service]
- ❸ Shonan-Shinjuku Line
- ❹ Keihin-Tohoku Line · Negishi Line
- ❺ Sagami Line
- ❻ Yokohama Line · Negishi Line
- ❼ Nambu Line
- ❽ Tsurumi Line
- ❾ Yamanote Line
- ❿ Chuo Line
- ⑪ Chuo Line [Rapid Service]
- ⑫ Chuo Line · Sobu Line [Local Train]
- ⑬ Chuo Line-Tozai Subway Line through service
- ⑭ Ome Line
- ⑮ Itsukaichi...
- ⑯ Hachiko L...
- ⑰ Utsunomi...
- ⑱ Takasaki...
- ⑲ Saikyo Li... through s...
- ⑳ Kawagoe...
- ㉑ Joban Lir...

© Copyright EAST JAPAN RAILWAY COMPANY
No reproduction nor republication without permission

JR EAST Railway Lines in Greater Tokyo

JR-EAST
2004.12.1